ANGLESEY RAILWAYS

Anglesey Railways

Geraint I. L. Jones

ISBN: 1-84527-006-1

Cover design: Sian Parri
Photographs: Geraint I. L. Jones; Anglesey Records Office

Published in 2005
by Gwasg Carreg Gwalch,
12 Iard yr Orsaf, Llanrwst, Wales LL26 0EH
01492 642031 01492 641502
books@carreg-gwalch.co.uk Website: www.carreg-gwalch.co.uk

GLOSSARY OF WELSH PLACE-NAMES

Holyhead	Caergybi
Anglesey	Ynys Môn
Holland Arms	Pentreberw
Red Wharf Bay	Traeth Coch
Salt Island	Ynys Halen
Menai Bridge	Porthaethwy
Barmouth	Y Bermo
Snowdonia	Eryri
Valley	Y Fali
Beaumaris	Biwmares
Newtown	Y Drenewydd
Neath	Castell-nedd
Brecon	Aberhonddu
Buckley	Bwcle
Flintshire	Sir y Fflint
Newborough	Niwbwrch
Menai Strait	Afon Menai
Amlwch Port	Porth Amlwch

CONTENTS

Introduction 9

Chapter 1:
BACKGROUND 11

Chapter 2:
THE CHESTER AND HOLYHEAD RAILWAY 13

Chapter 3:
THE ANGLESEY CENTRAL RAILWAY 42

Chapter 4:
THE PENTREBERW TO RED WHARF BAY LINE 76

Chapter 5:
OTHER ANGLESEY RAILWAY SCHEMES 87

Chapter 6:
THE HOLYHEAD MAIN LINE NOW 92

Chapter 7:
THE CENTRAL ANGLESEY LINE NOW 97

Chapter 8:
THE RED WHARF BAY LINE: 50 YEARS ON 102

Appendix: Technical Terms 107

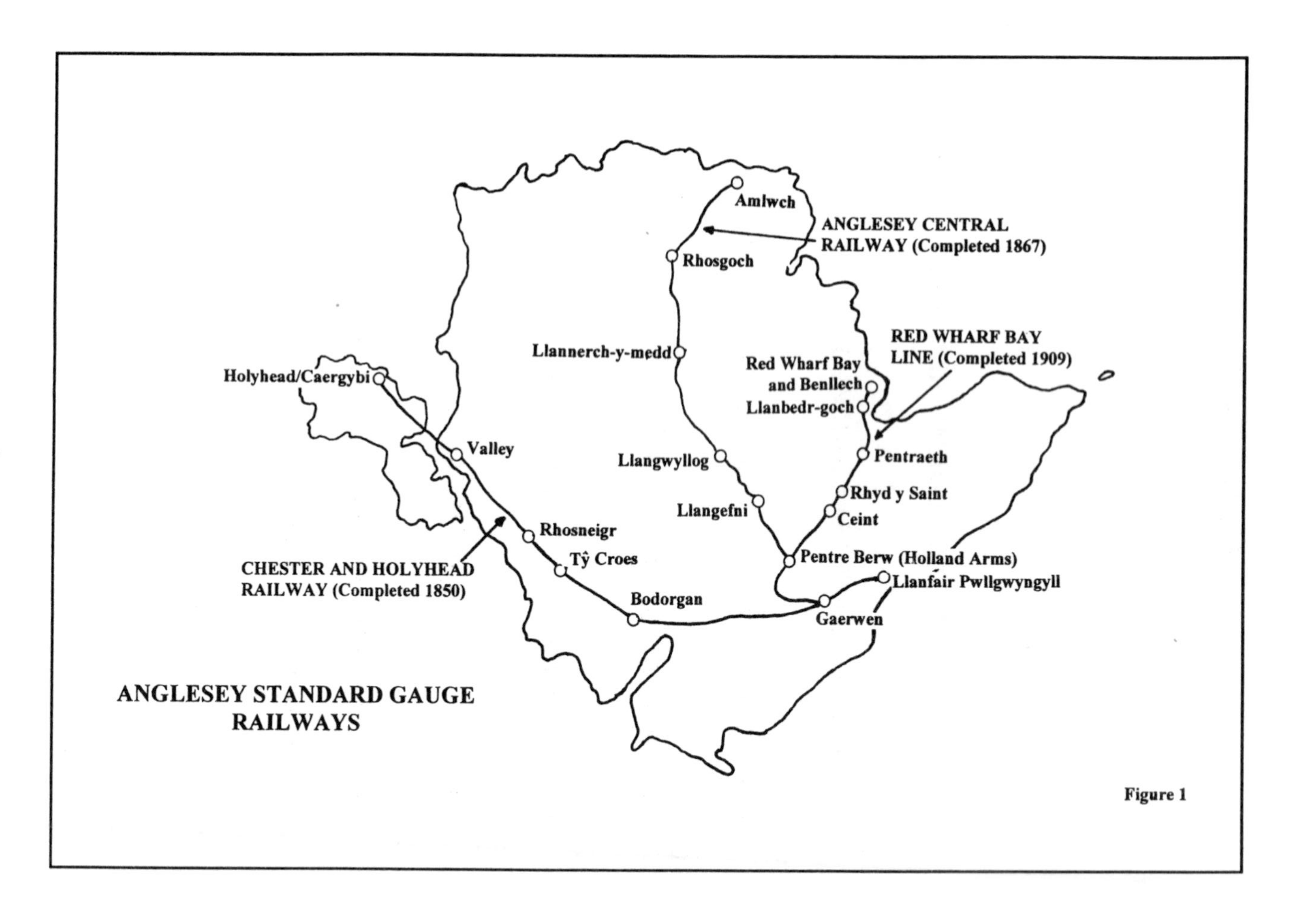
Amlwch
ANGLESEY CENTRAL
RAILWAY (Completed 1867)
Rhosgoch
RED WHARF BAY
LINE (Completed 1909)
Llannerch-y-medd
Red Wharf Bay
and Benllech
Llanbedr-goch
Holyhead/Caergybi
Valley
Llangwyllog
Pentraeth
Rhyd y Saint
Llangefni
Ceint
Rhosneigr
Tŷ Croes
Pentre Berw (Holland Arms)
Llanfair Pwllgwyngyll
CHESTER AND HOLYHEAD
RAILWAY (Completed 1850)
Bodorgan
Gaerwen
ANGLESEY STANDARD GAUGE
RAILWAYS

Figure 1

INTRODUCTION

The purpose of this small volume is to present in simple terms a short account of the building and development of the Anglesey Railway system. It does attempt to be a technical manual concerning the finer points of railway operation. It is intended for the layman who has an interest in the history of Anglesey's railways. Inevitably some technical terms are used, but these will be explained in the Appendix.

The 19th century was a period of unprecedented innovation and progress and this is reflected in the speed with which railways spread throughout Britain during this period. Three railways (Figure 1) were built in Anglesey: the Bangor to Holyhead main line, a part of the Chester to Holyhead Railway (completed 1850), the Central Anglesey Line (Gaerwen to Amlwch) (completed 1867), and finally the Holland Arms to Red Wharf Bay Line (completed 1909). An account of the construction of each line is given and each station is individually discussed and a track layout diagram is given. It should be remembered that track layouts are simply a guide – over the life of a station there could have been many changes. Some details of locomotives and rolling stock are included; however, it should be remembered that this is a specialist area and the details given here are not intended to be comprehensive. A number of publications dealing with this subject can be found.

Today, almost a century after the last of these lines was completed, much has happened. The last scheme to be completed, Holland Arms to Red Wharf, was the first to be closed and dismantled (1950). The Central Anglesey Line (also known as Lein Amlwch) was officially closed in 1964 following the Beeching Report of 1963. Miraculously, perhaps, the line (apart from some station buildings and sidings) still remains. The only railway line to have survived intact, albeit with somewhat depleted stations, is the main line to Holyhead.

All three Anglesey Railways now provide an interesting opportunity for today's railway enthusiast to discover the relics of times gone by on the island's railways and learn more about an interesting aspect of local history. This is discussed in Chapters 6-8.

Chapter 1
BACKGROUND

The Railways have been part of our lives for generations. We have witnessed their development, their growth as well as their decline, and in some cases, their demise. The history of the railway is linked to the Industrial Revolution which began in the 1770s. Industrialists turned to horses for their motive power as previous generations had always done. It is said that there was a shortage of horses in the 1790s, and that this was one of the main factors in the development of steam power.

Initially steam power was envisaged for use in collieries, quarries and other industrial applications. The first working steam-powered locomotive to run on fixed rails was said to have been built by Richard Trevithick (1771-1833) at Penydarren Ironworks, near Merthyr Tydfil in 1804. Its purpose was to convey iron from the works to a canal from where it was shipped by barge to the docks.

The first public railway worked by steam ran from Stockton-on-Tees to Darlington (County Durham) in 1825. The project engineer George Stephenson (1781-1848) drove the first train (powered by his engine Locomotion No. 1) along this single track railway. Stephenson won a prize for the innovative design of another of his locomotives, 'Rocket', in 1829. Amongst other early schemes was the Liverpool to Manchester Railway (1830) which used steam power on a 31 mile twin track. The Canterbury to Whitstable line in Kent is said to be the first to provide a regular steam passenger service. It opened on 3 May 1830.

During the next twenty years or so, railway companies sprang up virtually everywhere. It was quickly realised that fortunes were to be made and people flocked to invest. Every new railway scheme had to be examined and sanctioned by an Act of

Parliament. In 1845 alone, 620 such schemes were proposed and submitted for approval. 'Railway mania' was a phrase much used to describe the prevailing atmosphere in the mid-1840s. Inevitably perhaps, some schemes failed and many people lost money.

One question which had to be resolved as the railways expanded was the gauge (see Appendix). For most railways built after 1824, the gauge was standardised as 1435mm (4 ft. 8½in.); this was based on coal wagons used in the Tyneside area where early railway development took place. This is referred to as Standard Gauge – the main north Wales line and all Anglesey public railways were built to this specification.

The railway network, built by a considerable number of private companies had spread to serve most large towns and cities in mainland Britain by the mid-1840s. From main lines sprouted branch lines to serve smaller communities. By the late 1830s the main line system had reached north-west England. Inevitably it was to continue further west into north Wales so as to establish a connection with Ireland. It was by no means inevitable that Holyhead would have become the rail terminus and busy port that it now is. All that could have gone elsewhere. If so, the Britannia bridge would never have been built and Anglesey would never have had a main line railway – and quite possibly no public railways at all.

Chapter 2
CHESTER & HOLYHEAD RAILWAY

The so-called Irish Mail service first started in 1572, during the reign of Queen Elizabeth I. The Act of Union of 1800 had united Ireland with Great Britain and this inevitably resulted in a greater volume of shipping, passengers and mail crossing the Irish Sea from the mainland. The sum of £150,000 had been spent by the Government in improving the harbour at Holyhead between 1810 and 1824. This included the construction of the Admiralty Pier off Salt Island, which was 1150 feet (350 m) long and Moelfre stone was used in its exterior construction; a lighthouse was built at its end. In the 1820s the Irish Mail was being carried by horse-drawn coaches along roads which were often inadequate, although the bridges at Conwy and Menai Bridge had proved invaluable. During the 1840s it was, of course, inevitable that a railway would eventually be built across north Wales in order to take advantage of the increased traffic to Ireland and to operate the Irish Mail service. The railway would end at a suitable port, but Holyhead was not the only option.

It may seem strange to us now, but Porthdinllaen (on the Llŷn Peninsula) was also seen as a possible port for the operation of ferries to Ireland. In one way it seemed to be a better option since the north Wales railway would not have to cross the Menai Strait as it would if Holyhead were chosen.

In January 1836, a meeting was held at Caernarfon to support Porthdinllaen's case. Almost immediately, another public meeting was called by Sir Richard Bulkeley, Sir J.T. Stanley and others at the Penrhyn Arms, Bangor (where the University College of North Wales was later to be housed) on 12 February 1836 in favour of Holyhead. This was followed by other meetings in favour of Holyhead held in Anglesey and in Chester.

Two engineers named Charles Vignoles and John Urpeth Rastrick surveyed possible rail routes terminating at Porthdinllaen in 1836. Some of these routes involved steep gradients, but Vignoles recommended a route which ran to Porthdinllaen via Llangollen, Bala and Barmouth. He was of the opinion that the construction of a bridge over the Menai Strait was too great an undertaking. He was not in favour of a coastal rail route because construction of a railway between Bangor and Porthdinllaen would require a number of expensive tunnels and viaducts and make the scheme very costly.

Captain Francis Beaufort (1774-1857, famous for his scale of wind speeds) concluded in a report of December 1836 that Holyhead would be the ideal location but that building a railway to Holyhead would be impossible, so that Porthdinllaen was the only alternative. Vignoles obviously agreed with his conclusion.

It was reported that before the end of 1836 people were surveying in Anglesey for a proposed railway. In October 1838, at a meeting in the Penrhyn Arms, a Mr Francis Giles, a civil engineer, presented a report favouring the construction of a railway to Holyhead. He favoured using the existing Menai Suspension Bridge with carriages hauled by ropes over the bridge. Clearly the construction of a railway across the fairly flat lands of Anglesey was an easier proposition than constructing one through the more hilly areas of Snowdonia and the Llŷn Peninsula, even though the Menai Strait would present a tricky problem.

In December 1836, George Stephenson came to the conclusion that Holyhead was the preferred option; like Francis Giles he was in favour of rope haulage of carriages over Telford's Bridge. In May 1840, a Government committee favoured the coastal route of Giles and Stephenson.

The cost of the Chester to Holyhead line was estimated in 1839 to be £16,000 per mile. The people of Anglesey tried to persuade the Government to adopt this scheme, and a meeting was held in Holyhead to this effect in 1839. It was chaired by William Owen Stanley (Penrhos, Member of Parliament for Anglesey 1837-47) and present were Sir Richard Bulkeley (Baron Hill), Owen F. Meyrick (Bodorgan), Holland Griffith (Carreglwyd, Llanfaethlu) and others. In the meeting it was stated that no ship from Holyhead carrying letters to Ireland had sunk in nearly 100 years. In 1842, Sir Richard Bulkeley went as far as to hire a steamship to time the journey from Holyhead to Dublin. Even though there was considerable support for Holyhead and the construction of the railway, the necessary Railway Bill had still not been passed. Some of the delay might be explained by the recession of the late 1830s and early 1840s when money for ambitious and expensive projects was hard to find.

The original intention to haul carriages over Telford's Menai Suspension Bridge was dropped as in 1844 Robert Stephenson (1803-1859, the son of George Stephenson) was reported as saying that the bridge was not, in his opinion, strong enough to support the great weight of a train.

The Chester and Holyhead Railway Bill was presented to the House of Commons by William O. Stanley on 13 March 1844 and received Royal Assent on 4 July 1844. The Chester and Holyhead Railway Company was established with capital of £2,100,000 in £50 shares. The Government promised to spend £500,000 on Holyhead harbour. The London and Birmingham Railway contributed £1,000,000 to the company on the condition that 9 of the 18 directors on the board of the Chester and Holyhead Railway were appointed by them. Originally, the Grand Junction Railway (another powerful railway company of the time) had also promised support but withdrew. The Act permitted the construction of the railway from Chester to Holyhead except for a small section (about 4 miles in length from the west bank of Afon Ogwen to Llanfair Pwllgwyngyll and obviously including a bridge across the Menai Strait). The railway's engineer was Robert Stephenson and the station designs were by Francis Thompson. Before construction could begin, land needed to be purchased all along the north Wales coast and Anglesey. The entire length of the line was divided into a number of separate contracts. These contracts had to be agreed and workers found. Work on the railway began on 1 March 1845 at Bangor, Conwy and Chester. The contractor for the first 8 miles from Chester into north Wales was Edward Ladd Betts, a well-known railway contractor of the period.

The Chester and Holyhead Railway Completion Act received Royal Assent on 30 June 1845; it authorised the construction of the Afon Ogwen to Llanfair Pwllgwyngyll section (including the bridge).

Construction work on the railway in Anglesey began in mid-1845 in the parishes of Llangaffo and Trefdraeth. The contractor for this section (5.3 miles, 8.5 km) was also Edward Ladd Betts who held the contracts for the whole length of the line in Anglesey. Wooden sheds were set up near the works, and the villages of Llanfair Pwllgwyngyll, Gaerwen and Llangaffo grew considerably. A number of local families became wealthy through trade with the railway workers and the railway company.

In 1846, under an agreement between the Government and the Chester and Holyhead Railway Company (CHR), the railway company promised to pay £200,000 towards Holyhead harbour (a quarter of the estimated cost). The Government promised to pay the company £35,000 a year to carry mail and other goods on the railway. In 1850 the requirement to pay the sum of £200,000 was revoked because of the huge cost of building the Britannia bridge.

The CHR had initially ordered its own locomotives, but by 1846 the financial state of the company was giving cause for concern. In June 1847 an agreement was formulated between the CHR and the London and North Western Railway (LNWR) regarding the working of the line. Under this agreement the LNWR was to supply locomotives, rolling stock, train drivers and firemen, while the CHR was to supply station staff and engine sheds. Locomotives ordered by the CHR were to be taken over by the LNWR. The agreement was to be in force from the day the first services commenced, then unknown.

On 31 March 1848, a train travelled for the first time from Llanfair Pwllgwyngyll to Holyhead with directors, engineers and other dignitaries. Two locomotives had been brought to Holyhead by sea. Members of the public were given free rides on the following Saturday, but the line was not officially opened until 1 August 1848. The line from Chester to Bangor had been open since 1 May 1848, but since the bridge over the Menai Strait was not complete, passengers had to be carried by road from Bangor to

Llanfair Pwllgwyngyll across Telford's suspension bridge. The first Irish Mail train left Euston at 8:45 p.m. on 31 July 1848 and reached Bangor at 5:25 a.m. on 1 August. After road transportation over Telford's bridge, it then continued from Llanfair Pwllgwyngyll to Holyhead, arriving there late at 9 a.m. On the same day, the CHR's four paddle steamers began operation. By this time, however, the Government had given the sea mail contract to another company.

On the Holyhead line stations were situated at Llanfair Pwllgwyngyll, Bodorgan, Tŷ Croes, Valley and Holyhead itself. Gaerwen station was an afterthought; Mr W. Bulkeley Hughes, a well-known local figure, had organised a petition for a station to be built. Gaerwen station is about half a mile to the south of the village and very near to Llanddaniel Fab. Although a station at Llangaffo had been planned, it was never built apparently because of difficulties caused by some landowners.

The total length of the line from the Menai Strait to Holyhead is just over 22 miles (35 km). It runs parallel to the A5 for a few miles, and before reaching Gaerwen runs to the south of the island towards the flatter areas near Malltraeth and Aberffraw. Before reaching Holyhead it nears the A5 once more near Valley, and the railway and A5 cross the Stanley Embankment (Pont Lasinwen) together to reach Holy Island. The Stanley Embankment is 1300 yards (1190 m) long and was built by Thomas Telford as part of the A5 between 1815 and 1819. The embankment was widened to accommodate the railway and the wall between the line and the road was apparently erected so that horses would not be startled by the locomotives. There are two tunnels on the line (near Trefdraeth) which are 413 yards (378 m) long (Grid Reference SH 400 697) and 115 yards (105 m) long (Grid Reference SH 396 698). These tunnels are officially known as Bodorgan No.1 and Bodorgan No.2 respectively. Nearby there is a viaduct (Grid Reference SH 420 690) with 19 arches which crosses the Malltraeth marshes.

Some local people were dismayed to discover that the new railway failed to serve many of the more populated parts of the island. For example, it passed nowhere near the market town of

Llangefni, but instead passed through the very rural southern part of Anglesey, which then, as now, was comparatively thinly populated.

The Chester to Holyhead line was not complete, however, as the bridge across the Menai Strait was still to be completed. The work of designing the bridge had been entrusted to Robert Stephenson. His original design was a kind of viaduct with two arches carrying the railway about 100 feet (31m) above the Straits. There were fears that this was not high enough and that ships could collide with the arches. Eventually Stephenson came up with the tubular concept.

Essentially the bridge took the form of metal tubes resting on stone supports, one at either end of the bridge (abutments) and three towers (Figures 2a and 2b). The central tallest tower stands on a rocky islet (Craig y Fyrdan or Britannia Rock) in the Straits but the other two towers are land based. The bridge is actually two tubes (one for each of the railway tracks), each in four sections. Therefore eight tubes needed to be constructed; four of these (the water tubes, i.e. the ones between the Britannia Tower and the two side towers) were built on site on the mainland side of the Straits. They would then need to be hoisted to their places between the towers. The total height of the central Britannia tower above the Straits is about 230 feet (70 m), the trains being carried through the tubes 103 ft (31 m) above high water level.

In August 1845, a structural engineer and mathematician named Eaton Hodgkinson helped Robert Stephenson with a number of experiments to determine the best form of the tubes. Tubes of cylindrical, elliptical and rectangular section were tested, and the results of these experiments showed that rectangular tubes in wrought iron were the most satisfactory. William Fairbairn (a shipbuilder as well as a civil engineer) constructed a one-sixth scale model of the bridge in order to more accurately test its rigidity and strength. The tube model weighed 5 tons and was 75 feet long and 2½ feet wide. Inside the tube were cellular compartments running the length of the tube. The tests showed that this was the strongest and most rigid form of construction.

The designs for the masonry supports were completed by

Figure 2a

BRITANNIA BRIDGE
(Schematic diagram, not to scale)

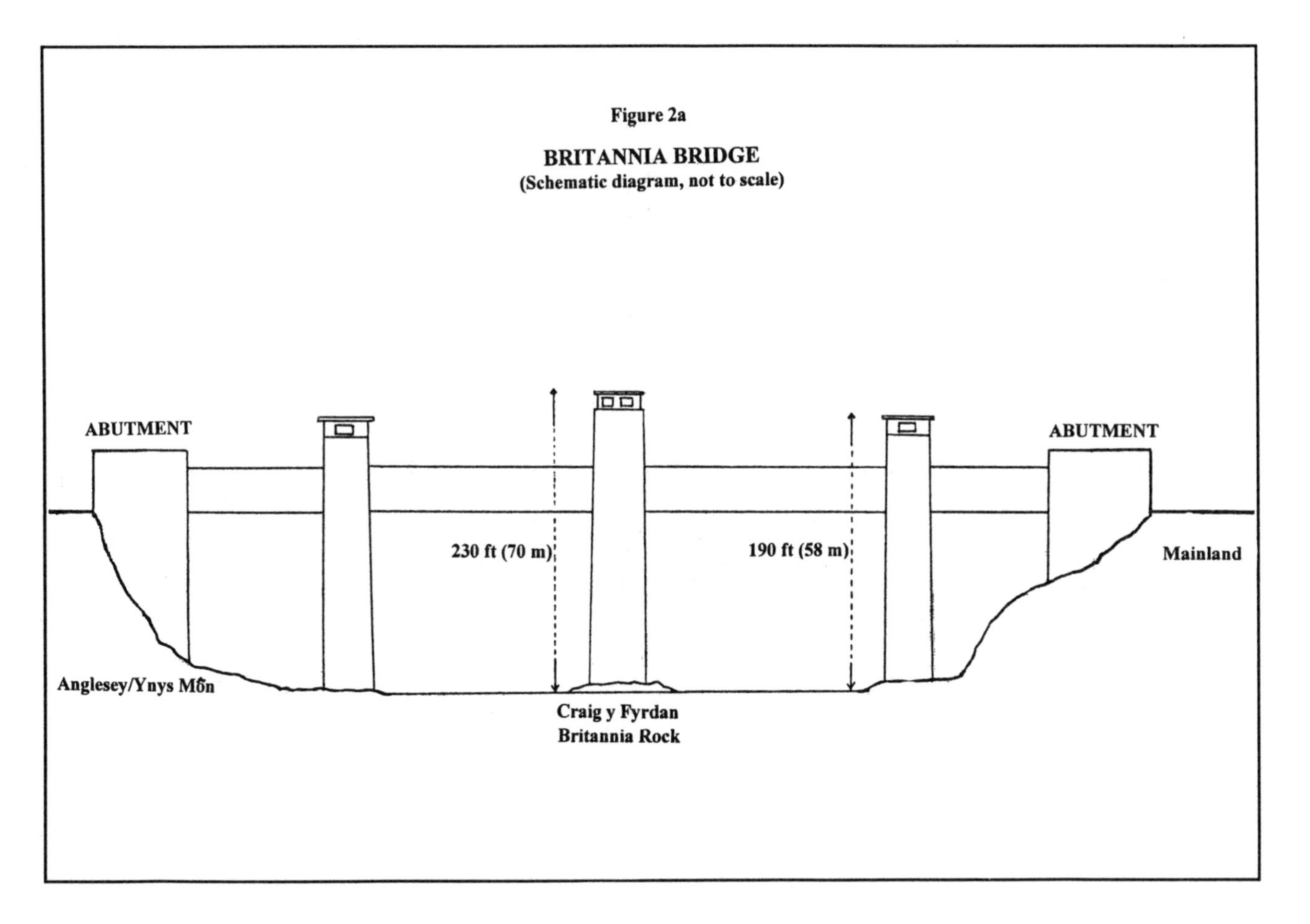

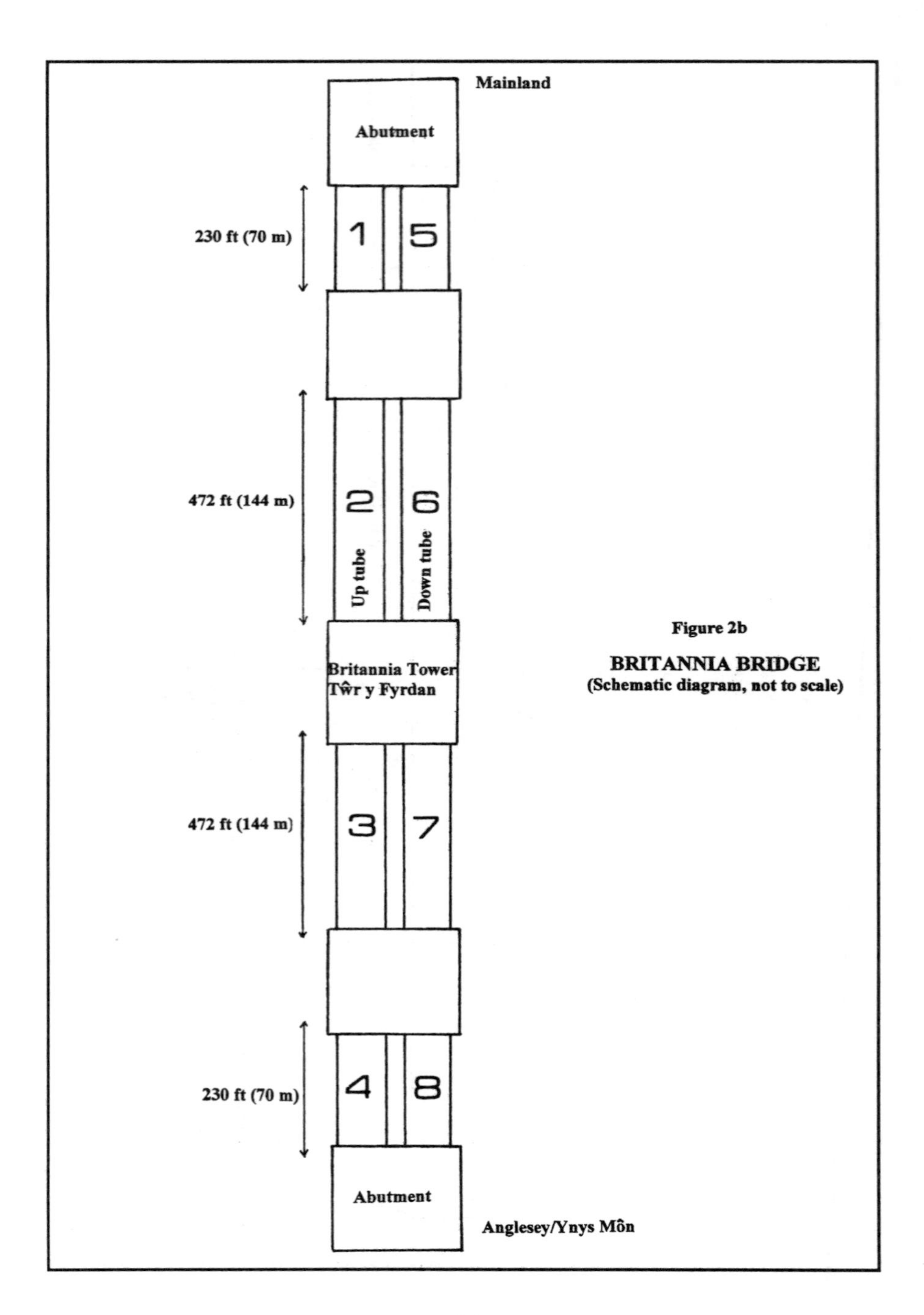

Figure 2b

BRITANNIA BRIDGE
(Schematic diagram, not to scale)

Francis Thompson in February 1846 and a joint tender from John Hemingway, Benjamin J. Nowell and Charles Pearson for the sum of £130,000 was accepted. The construction was to be supervised by Stephenson's assistant Edwin Clark. Accommodation was built nearby for the workers in the form of 80 cottages, shops, and even a school. Work on the stone supports began on Craig y Fyrdan (Britannia Rock) on 17 March 1847, and the last stone was laid by Stephenson himself on 22 June 1849. Stone from Penmon was used for the main external work on the supports as it would withstand the effects of exposure to the sea much better than most rocks. The interior stonework was of Runcorn sandstone. Grooves were left on both sides of the centre tower and on one side of the others in order to facilitate the positioning of the metal tubes.

Work on constructing the tubes began on 10 April 1846. The full-size tubes were constructed of wrought iron of rectangular section with cellular compartments at the top and bottom in accordance with the scale model tests. It was this feature which gave the tubes their immense strength; Stephenson's innovative design was the forerunner of a construction method now used very widely – the box girder bridge. Each of the longer tube sections was 472 ft (144 m) long and weighed 1500 tons. The smaller tubes were 230 ft (70 m) long. The total weight supported by the three towers and two abutments estimated to be approximately 10,500 tons. The tubes were to be fixed on the Britannia tower but to rest on rollers on the other towers and the abutments in order to allow for expansion and contraction. The total length of the bridge was 1494 feet (455 m). By November 1848, construction of the four water tubes (Figure 2b: nos. 2,3,6,7) were virtually complete.

These tubes were to be floated out onto the Menai Strait, and hoisted into position. The land tubes (Figure 2b: nos. 1,4,5,8) between the side towers and the abutments, on the other hand, were built in their place supported by timber platforms and scaffolding. The mode of raising the water tubes was suggested by the engineers Edwin Clark and William Fairbairn. This was the challenging part of the construction process; Stephenson himself was a very conservative person, and being at the cutting edge of

1840s technology was not to his taste! He endured many sleepless nights and much anxiety, and he was constantly plagued by thoughts of failure. He had sought to refine the process of floating out the tubes to the required positions by the use of a scale model.

On 20 June 1849, the first of the tubes for the Up line (Figure 2b: no. 3) was finally positioned after two failed attempts the previous day. Pontoons were placed under the tube, and the incoming tide floated it and carried it aided by cables and winches. So strong were the currents in the Staits that this operation could only be carried out at the times when the tide turned. Stephenson himself stood on top of the tube and directed operations, watched by a crowd said to number thousands. Many spectators had arrived by train such was the excitement. The flamboyant engineer Isambard Kingdom Brunel (1806 – 1859), a personal friend of Stephenson, was present to witness the operation. As the delicate operation got underway, a capstan suddenly gave way and a number of men were thrown into the water. The spectators were called to help, and eventually the tube was brought to rest in the appropriate grooves. It must have come as an immense relief to Stephenson to see his ambitious theory turned into reality. The tube was hoisted by giant hydraulic jacks starting on 20 August 1849. A few days later when the tube had been raised by 24 feet (6.1 m) the hydraulic jack in the Anglesey tower failed causing the tube to fall. Fortunately Stephenson had taken the precaution of placing packing under the tube as it was moved upwards, and it fell only a few inches. Unfortunately, one man was killed and the tube suffered minor damage. The damage was quickly repaired and the lifting operation restarted on 1 October, and on 11 November 1849 the tube was in position.

The second of the water tubes for the Up line (Figure 2b: no.2) was positioned on 2 December 1849 and raised to its place by 7 January 1850. The remaining two land tubes (Figure 2b: nos. 1 and 4) to house the Up line were completed and all the Up tubes joined together by 5 March 1850 when a train (powered by three locomotives named *Pegasus, Cambrian* and *St David*) was used by Stephenson early in the morning to test the bridge. Later that day Stephenson ceremonially placed the last rivet in its place, and the same locomotives carried Stephenson and several hundred others (in over 30 carriages) as well as 45 coal wagons across the bridge. It was inspected and opened to the public for the first time on 18 March 1850. On that afternoon a train travelled from Holyhead to Chester for the first time. The bridge was therefore operational but with the Up line only in use.

Between June and August 1850 the Down line water tubes (Figure 2b: nos. 6 and 7) were floated out and raised. The complete bridge with its twin tracks was inspected on 19 October 1850 and was officially declared open on 21 October 1850. From the 1870s onwards, a covering (or canopy) of tarred canvas was placed over the tubes, and this covering remained, in various forms, until the disastrous 1970 fire. The metal rails within the tubes were placed on timber supports. The bridge was meticulously kept rust-free by continuous painting, using paint containing sand.

A banquet in honour of Robert Stephenson was held on 21 August 1851 in a marquee near the George Hotel, Bangor (later the George site of the Normal College) in the presence of Lord Pennant M.P. as well as a number of other dignitaries and members of Parliament. In October 1852, Queen Victoria, Prince Albert and the young Prince of Wales visited the bridge and were shown round by Robert Stephenson. In 1859 Robert Stephenson died; it is said that he had been prematurely aged by the stress of his work. Brunel, his friend and rival, also died a comparatively young man at about the same time.

The Britannia bridge proved to be immensely strong – much stronger than anyone had imagined. For Stephenson it was a triumph; it confirmed his position as one of Britain's best civil engineers. In common with so many construction projects of the time, there were deaths caused by accidents. In a prominent position in St Mary's Church cemetery at Llanfair Pwllgwyngyll (Grid Reference SH 537 712), a short distance from the bridge, stands a memorial to those who lost their lives during its construction. There are 18 names on the memorial, including that of a five year old girl.

A number of other accidents occurred as a result of fighting among some of the construction workers particularly, it is said, among the Irishmen. In 1847, the contractors on the Anglesey side, Messrs Nowell and Company, hired two additional policemen and forty workers were said to have been sacked because of their 'disgraceful conduct' on Sundays. A minister, the Rev. T. Jackson, was appointed to work among the men as a kind of missionary. There were reports of thefts of goods during the night and as a result the company was forced to recruit security staff. One of these security men, John Rowlands aged 30, was murdered in 1848; a man was taken into custody on suspicion of his murder, but was later released because there was insufficient evidence against him.

The building of the railway across the island as well as other large works at Holyhead were the most ambitious construction projects ever seen in Anglesey. Hundreds were employed and perhaps it was inevitable that some trouble would occur. At one stage workers on the Holyhead section of the line went on strike so as to secure a pay increase. A particularly ugly incident occurred in Holyhead in 1851 (after the railway was complete but other works at Holyhead were still in progress). Some workers from Denbighshire and Flintshire (not native Anglesey men) rose against Irishmen who were staying there. Some of the Irishmen were forced to flee to their own country on board a ship called the *Cambria*.

By this time the construction of the railway was over and a number of men were unemployed and even receiving financial help from parish sources. The magistrates were reportedly kept busy by the numbers of thieves. Irishmen and other strangers seemed to be on the receiving end of much of the blame. The parishioners of Llanfihangel Ysgeifiog (Gaerwen) were reported to be complaining bitterly about the behaviour of beggars in their community.

After completion of the bridge, which cost well in excess of £600,000, the CHR was in very deep financial trouble. Four stone lions which guard the bridge entrance had been in position since 1849; these were the work of Gloucestershire sculptor John Thomas. They are about 30 feet (9.1 m) long and they are said to weight over 80 tons each. There was also the intention to place a large statue of Britannia on the centre tower of the bridge as a final finishing touch to the whole project. This did not prove to be possible such was the financial situation. The company had received a considerable blow in 1846 when it lost the contract to carry mail to Dublin. In 1850 the CHR was placed on lease to the financially stronger company the LNWR who ran the line from the outset. Before the end of 1850, the equipment used to build the Britannia bridge was sold for considerable sums. The hydraulic jacks were purchased by the company that manufactured them, and were shown in the Great Exhibition at the Crystal Palace in London in 1851. On 13 October 1852, Queen Victoria, Prince Albert and the Prince of Wales visited the site of the bridge.

On a cold December day in 1848, in the first few months of the line's operation, when the Anglesey section was still separated from the mainland, a young mother and her baby were given permission to travel on a locomotive to Holyhead. She was apparently the wife of a railway labourer. When the train was a few miles from its destination, the engine's boiler system developed a fault and the woman and her baby were both killed, being scalded by hot steam. Such tragedies were fortunately rare. Another accident in the same area in October 1861 was caused by a defective wheel. No-one was killed but three carriages were derailed.

On 1 January 1859, the debts and liabilities of the CHR were taken over by the Euston-based LNWR. This company continued until 1923, when railways in Britain were reorganised. The LNWR then became part of the LMSR (London, Midland and Scottish Railways). When the railway network was nationalised on 1 January 1948 (as a result of the Transport Act 1947), the north Wales lines became part of the London Midland region of the newly-created British Railways. In the 1960s extensive electrification of the London to Holyhead main line was carried out, but the north Wales section has never been electrified, and therefore relied on Diesel locomotives after steam services were withdrawn. In 1964 it was reported that upgrading of the track within the tubes of the Britannia bridge took place. In the late 1960s the bridge was subjected to a detailed technical inspection to ensure that it was strong enough to handle freightliner trains for the transport of containers to and from Ireland. The bridge was found to be in very good condition.

LOCOMOTIVES AND ROLLING STOCK

In the early years of the line's operation by the LNWR, Trevithick locomotives of the 'Crewe' type were used: 2-2-2 locomotives for passenger services and 2-4-0 for freight services. In the 1850s locomotives of the 'Raven' class named *Pegasus* (not the engine of the same name used by Stephenson on the day of the Britannia bridge's opening) and *Cerberas* were stationed at Holyhead. In the 1860s 2-2-2 locomotives of the 'Lady of the Lake' class were introduced and worked on the line for many years. The same decade saw the introduction of the 'Newton' class of 2-4-0 locomotives, designed by Ramsbottom of the LNWR. The 1870s saw the introduction of the 'Precedent' class 2-4-0 locomotives designed by Francis William Webb, chief mechanical engineer of the LNWR. These gradually replaced the 'Lady of the Lake' class, and were in reliable service well into the twentieth century. The Webb-designed 2F 0-6-2T (despite its classification, used widely for passenger and freight operation) and 1P 2-4-2T locomotives (see Appendix) were used extensively on the line from the early 1880s onwards. These engines gave extremely long service, with some still in use after World War 2. Aspinall Class 27 3F 0-6-0 locomotives (see Appendix) were first introduced in the 1890s and also gave long service.

Early in the twentieth century, locomotives of various classes including 'Precursor', 'George the Fifth' and 'Prince of Wales' were in service over many years. The period between the two World Wars saw an increase in passenger traffic and almost a hundred passenger trains on parts of the line every week. From the early 1930s the new Royal Scot Class 7P 4-6-0 locomotives (see Appendix) took the Irish Mail, and this locomotive was very widely used for over twenty years. Also in the 1930s the Stanier-designed 'Black Five' 5MT 4-6-0 (see Appendix) was introduced and was used for passenger and freight services for many years.

From 1946 Ivatt 2MT 2-6-2T locomotives (see Appendix) were introduced and extensively used in north Wales. They replaced the ageing LNWR 2-4-2T and 0-6-2T locomotives.

From the early 1950s, Princess Coronation Pacific 8P 4-6-2 locomotives and the new BR Britannia Pacific 7P6F 4-6-2 locomotives (see Appendix) took over. DMUs (see Appendix) were used almost entirely for local trains from the mid-1960s, but main line express trains continued with steam locomotives until 1967. In the 1980s diesel power included Class 40, Class 45, Class 31, Class 33 and Class 47 locomotives. In the 1990s Class 158 DMUs were introduced.

In the late 1980s and early 1990s, steam specials ran on the north Wales line and on to Anglesey. The preserved locomotives used included the LMSR Stanier 'Princess Royal' Class 8P 4-6-2 *Princess Elizabeth,* and the BR Standard Class 8P 4-6-2 *Duke of Gloucester*.

In the early days of the Chester and Holyhead Railway, railway carriages were fairly small with 4 or 6 wheels. First class carriages were lit by oil lamps from 1848. The more modern larger carriages with 8 wheels were not introduced until 1883. The Irish Mail was the first train to be lit by gas in 1862, and equipment for supplying the gas was installed at Holyhead. This was very quickly discontinued (reverting back to oil) but gas lamps reappeared on a regular basis in 1875. Sleeping carriages were first introduced on the route in 1875 and were based on the existing six-wheeled carriages. More modern purpose-built sleeping carriages appeared in 1891. The Irish Mail and express trains were fitted with the more efficient vacuum brakes in 1882.

THE STATIONS

Llanfair Pwllgwyngyll (Grid Reference SH 526 716)
This station (initially known officially as Llanfair) which is 0.9 mile (1.4 km) from the Britannia bridge was opened in 1848, but was burnt down on 13 November 1865. A new station building was constructed shortly afterwards. Before the opening of the Britannia

Bridge when the Anglesey line was operated separately, the station had a locomotive shed. After the bridge was completed, the shed was considered unnecessary and was removed in 1851. The station had a signal box (near a level crossing), a footbridge and a small goods yard which handled a range of goods (including flour and animal feeds) and some livestock (Figure 3). The station had the distinction of having a turntable which was used to feed wagons (not locomotives) into different sidings. The station also had a 20-ton weighbridge for lorries. The Llanfair Pwllgwyngyll station was closed in February 1966, but after the disastrous fire on the Britannia Bridge in 1970, it became a temporary terminus with a wooden platform on 29 May 1970. After services were restored, it closed on 31 January 1973 but was officially reopened (and officially named Llanfairpwll) with two new (shorter) platforms on 7 May 1973. The Station House was sold to the Pringle Company in 1986 and restored by them in 1994; it was spruced up prior to a visit by the Queen in 2002. Some local services used to stop at Llanfair Pwllgwngyll; more recently it has become a request stop only.

Gaerwen (Grid Reference SH 485 708)
This station, 3.7 miles (5.9 km) from the Britannia bridge, was opened in January 1849 and enlarged in the early 1870s in response to increased traffic (Figure 4). There were two signal boxes in Gaerwen, both on the Up side. Number 1 Box controlled the gates of the level crossing, points and signals on the Llanfair Pwllgwyngyll side. This box is still in place. Number 2 Box controlled train movements to and from the Amlwch branch line and was taken out of use in 1967. Gaerwen station had a bay platform (see Appendix) for use by trains from the Amlwch branch line. After the LNWR acquired the Amlwch line in 1876, an improved junction with the main line was built. There was a goods yard handling considerable quantities of agricultural materials and coal merchants were based there. The station closed to passenger traffic in 1966, but coal was transported here up to 1984. It is currently completely out of use, the only one of the main line stations to permanently close.

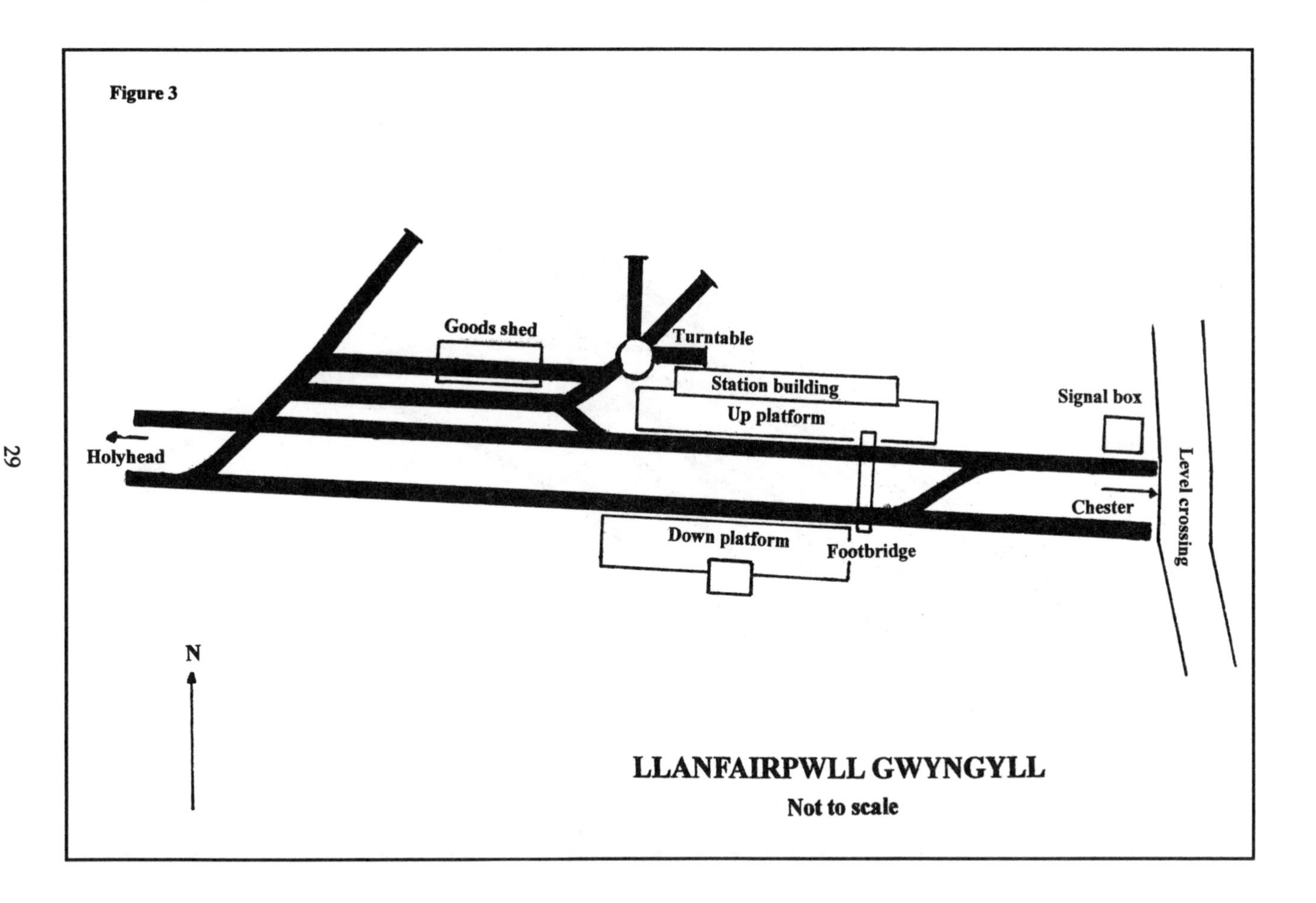
Goods shed
Turntable
Station building
Up platform
Signal box
Holyhead
Level crossing
Chester
Down platform
Footbridge
N
LLANFAIRPWLL GWYNGYLL
Not to scale

Figure 3

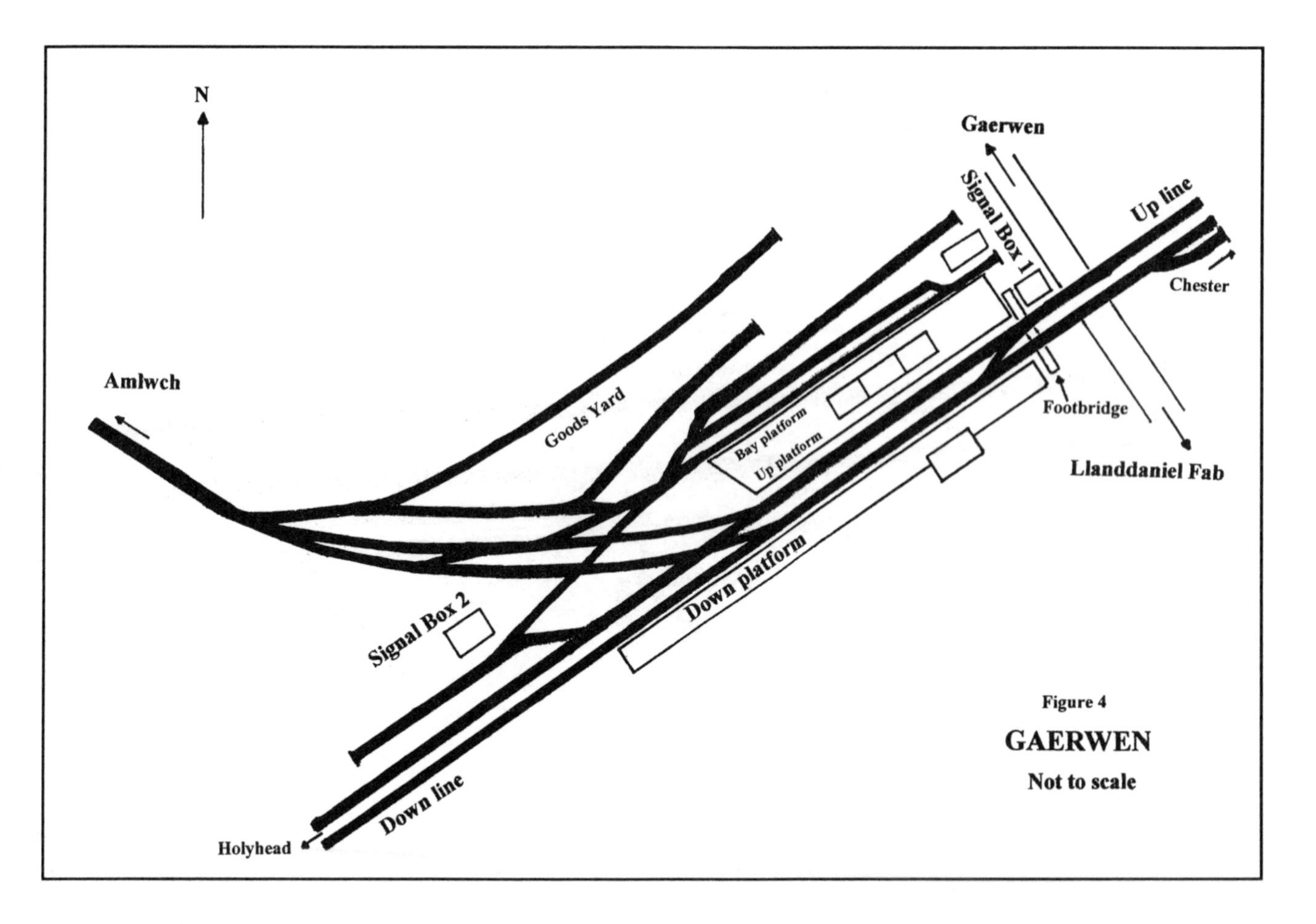

Figure 4
GAERWEN
Not to scale

Bodorgan (Grid Reference SH 387 702)
This station (Figure 5), which is 10.2 miles (16.3 km) from the Britannia bridge, was originally to be called Trefdraeth, and was opened in October 1849. There was originally a small signal box in the centre of the Down platform. There was a fairly small goods yard which handled livestock, coal etc. The goods yard closed in December 1964, and the station is now a request stop for some passenger services.

Tŷ Croes (Grid Reference SH 348 724)
This station (Figure 6) was originally designated as Llanfaelog, but opened as Tŷ Croes in November 1848. It is 12.9 miles (20.6 km) from the Britannia bridge. A signal box was added in 1872 to replace a previous hut. This box still stands next to the level crossing. The Up and Down platforms are on opposite sides of this crossing. A small goods yard handled livestock. There was a warehouse and a crane. The goods yard was closed in December 1964, and the station now serves as a request stop for some passenger services.

Rhosneigr (Grid Reference SH 328 738)
Rhosneigr (Figure 7) was not one of the original stations on the Chester and Holyhead Railway. It was opened on 1 May 1907, and its intention was to cash in on Rhosneigr's development as a tourist resort. It is 15 miles (24 km) from the Britannia bridge. Originally the station was provided with wooden huts. During the First World War it was closed from January 1917 to February 1919 as an economy measure. The wooden station buildings were replaced by concrete structures (of unusual design) on the Up and Down platforms in 1953. Rhosneigr is easily the simplest station on the line, with no sidings or a goods yard. There was no signal box, but signals to protect the station were operated by lever frames (see Appendix). Rhosneigr is now a request stop for some passenger services. It is interesting to note that, in 1921, sidings were constructed 1.1 miles (1.8 km) north of Rhosneigr station at Trewan Sands crossing (Grid Reference SH 319 753) for the purpose of extracting sand used by locomotives to assist braking.

Figure 5

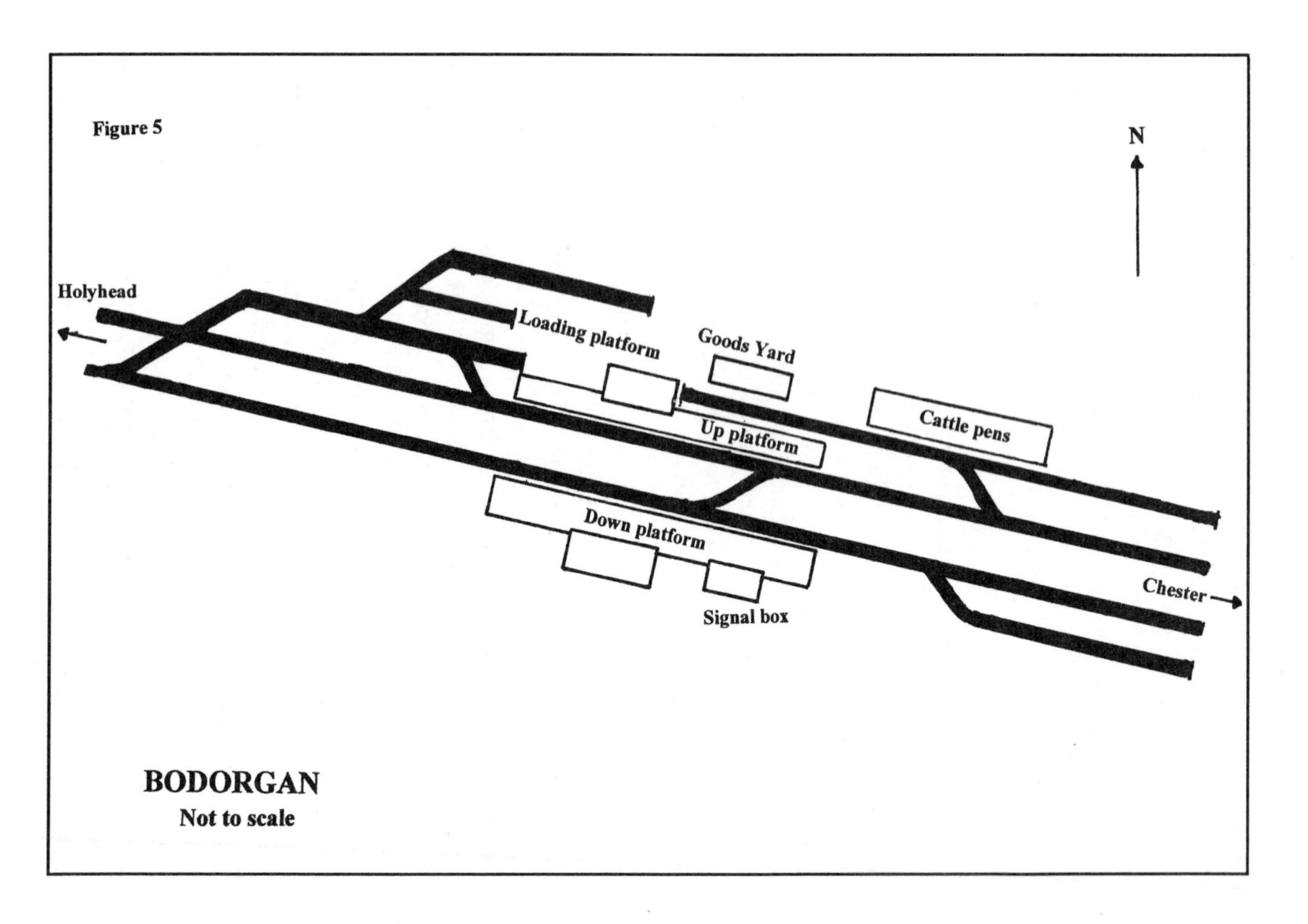
N
Holyhead
Loading platform
Goods Yard
Cattle pens
Up platform
Down platform
Signal box
Chester
BODORGAN
Not to scale

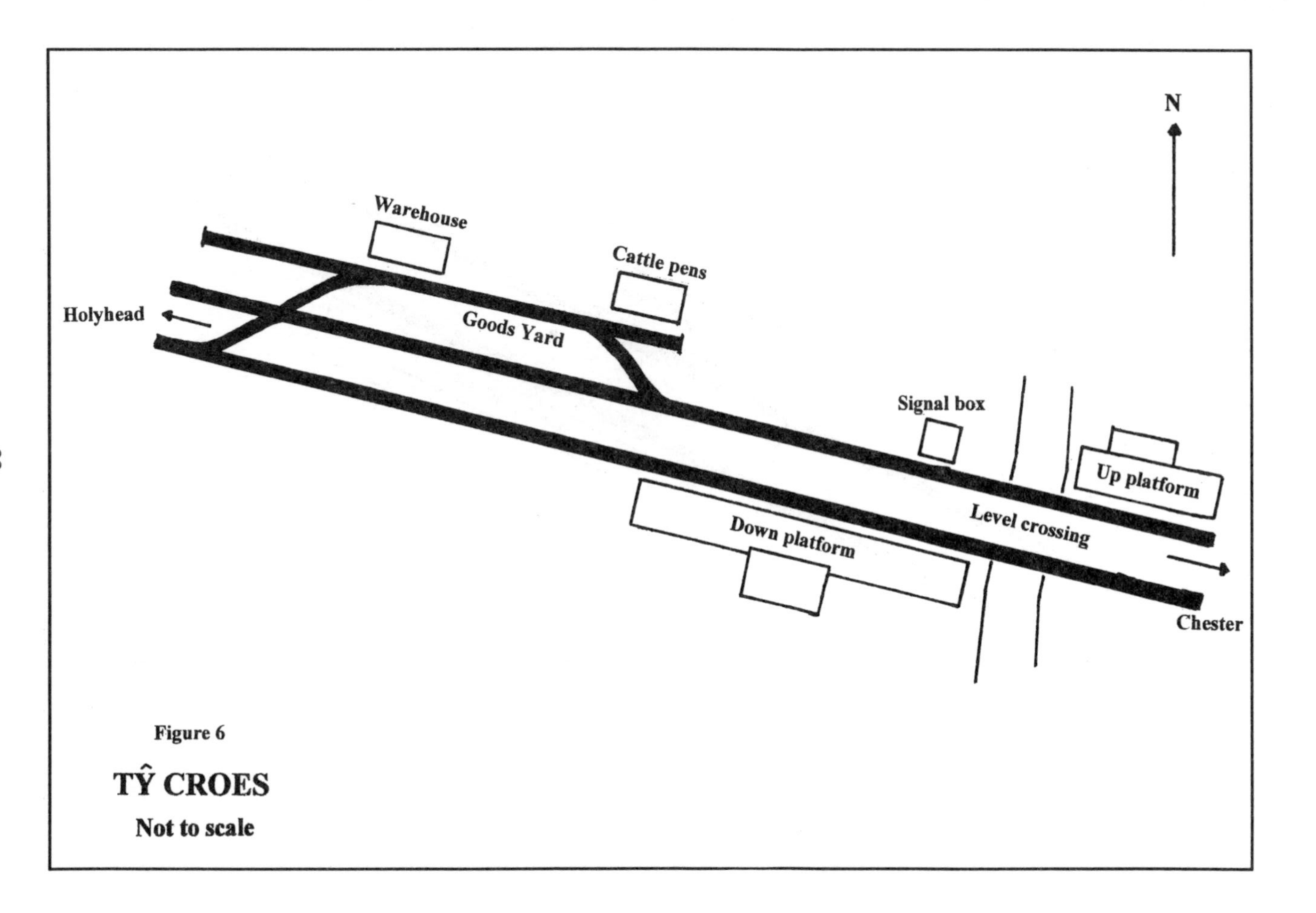

Figure 6
TŶ CROES
Not to scale

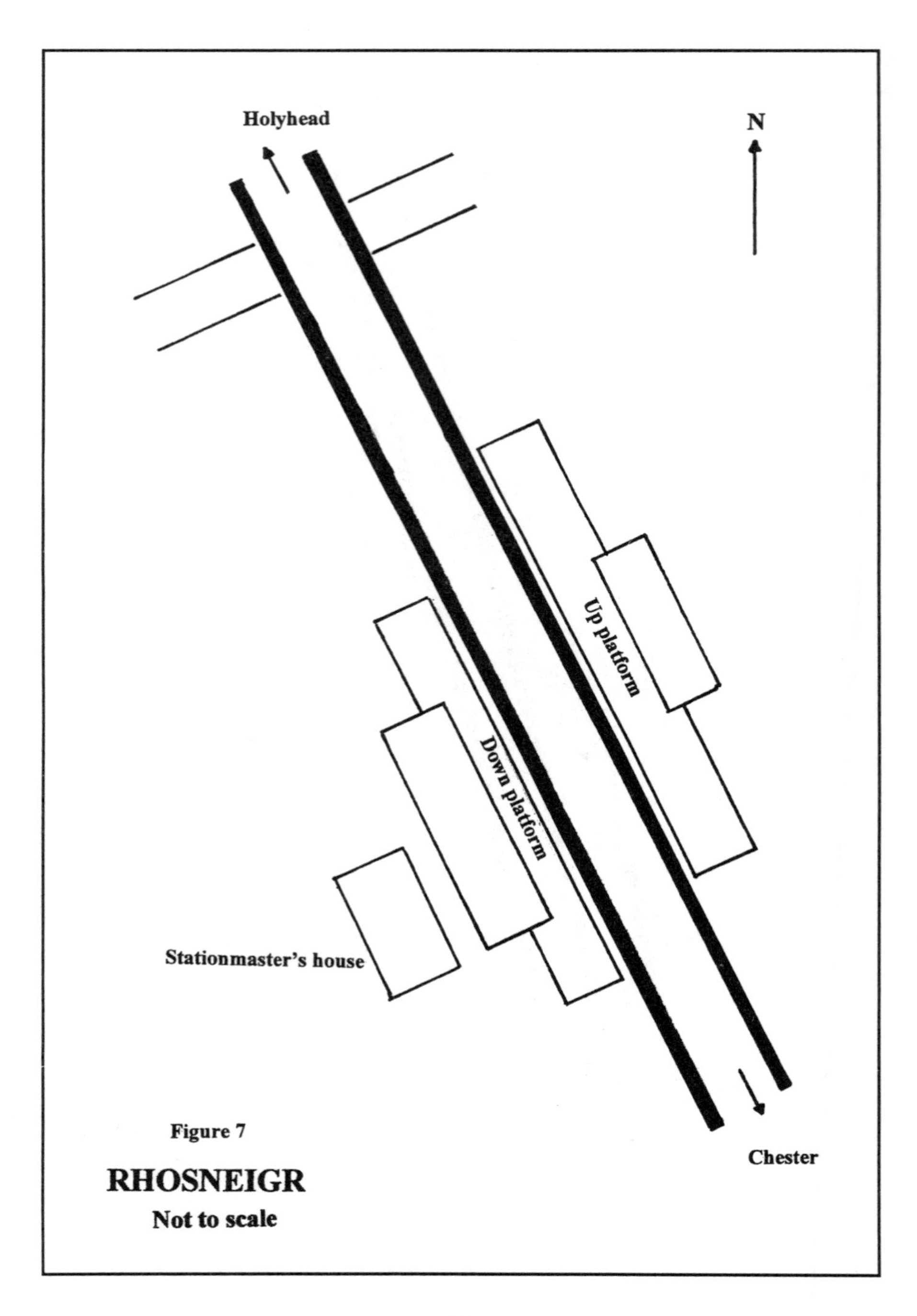

Figure 7

RHOSNEIGR

Not to scale

Valley (Grid Reference SH 292 792)

The Valley station (Figure 8) opened in October 1849 and is 19 miles (30.4 km) from the Britannia bridge. The station buildings were slightly extended in 1870 and the platforms lengthened in 1889. There was a signal box near the level crossing. A goods yard handled livestock and various commodities. One siding served a corn mill. It closed in February 1966, but was reopened for some passenger services in 1982. Currently some passenger trains stop at Valley by request only. In 1962 a siding was constructed south of the station for transporting materials to the Wylfa Power Station. This was used until 1988 by a haulage company involved with transporting goods to Ireland. An additional part to this siding was installed in 1989 for turning steam locomotives (Figure 9). Valley station continued to handle nuclear flasks for Wylfa. About 1.5 miles (2.4 km) from Valley station towards Holyhead, a siding was installed for the Anglesey Aluminium Company. This was used for the transportation of materials to and from the site, including coke which is used by the plant in large quantities.

Holyhead (Grid Reference SH 247 823)

The first temporary station was located near Porth Dafarch Road (Figure 10). The CHR Holyhead Extension Bill of 1847 gave the CHR the power to build an extension (1.29 miles, 2.06 km) from the existing line to the proposed packet pier where a station was to be built. This extension involved a tunnel 490 feet (124 m) long. North of the tunnel a branch (0.7 miles, 1.05 km) was to reach the Admiralty Pier. However these proposals were never implemented.

On 20 May 1851, a 0.7 mile (1.1 km) single track extension (mostly on a timber viaduct) was opened to Admiralty Pier (completed 1821) and a new Holyhead station came into use at the south end of the railway's inner harbour in September 1851. It was 22.3 miles (35.7 km) from the Britannia bridge. At first the Admiralty Pier extension was worked by horses, but by the end of the 1850s improvements had been carried out and 0-4-0 tank locomotives were used. There was also a station at the Admiralty Pier, opened in 1851 and closed to passenger traffic in 1925.

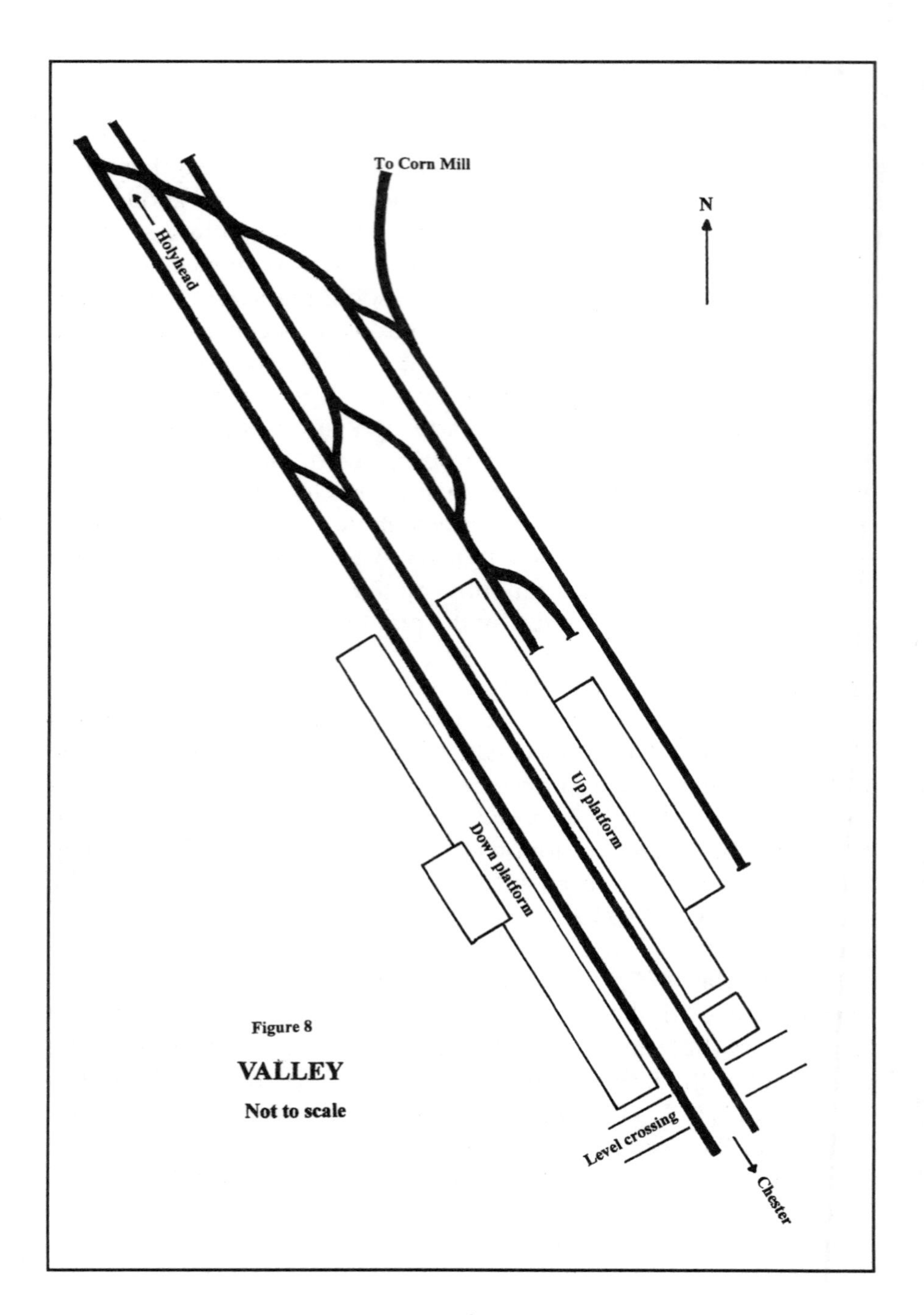

Figure 8

VALLEY

Not to scale

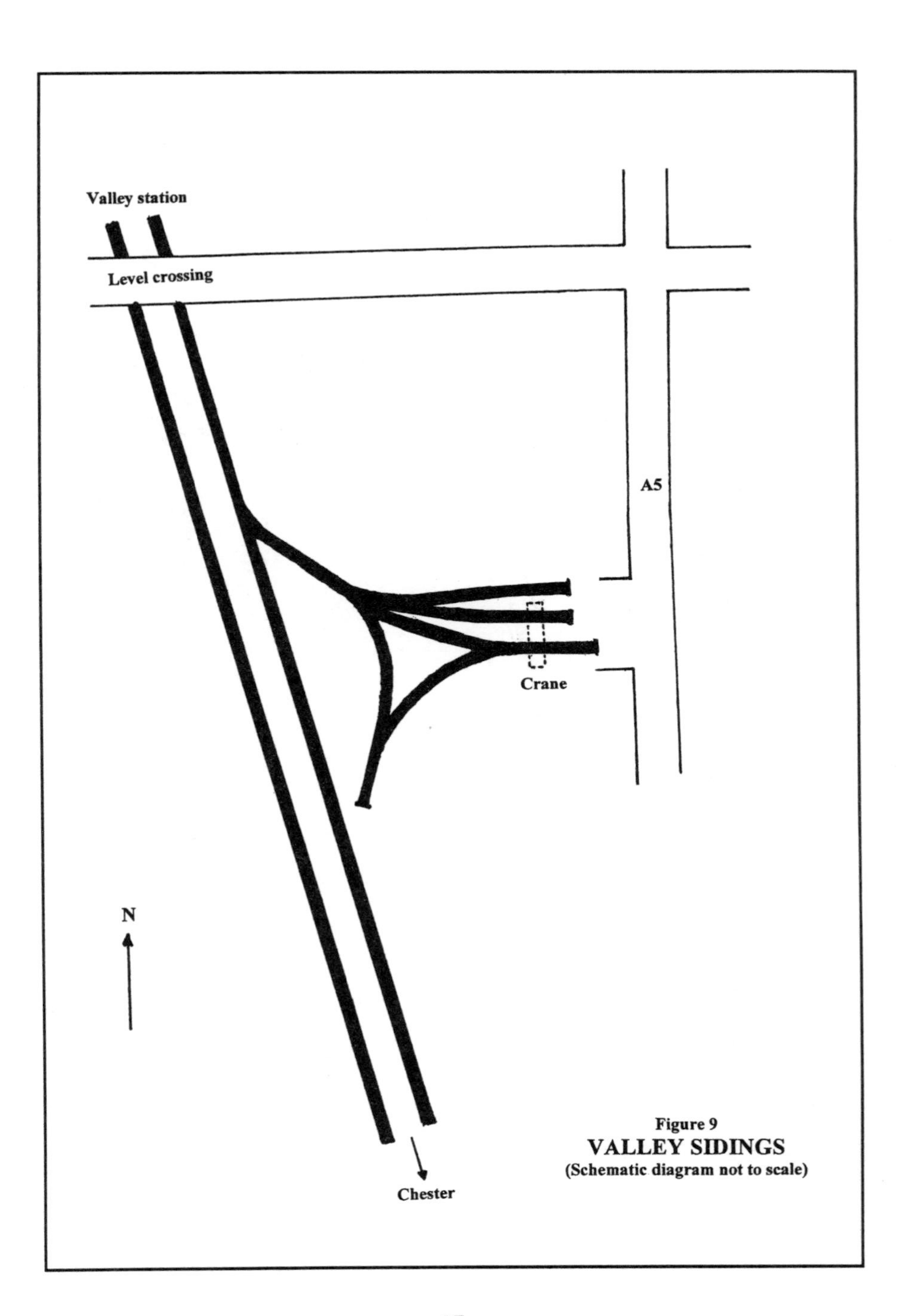

Figure 9
VALLEY SIDINGS
(Schematic diagram not to scale)

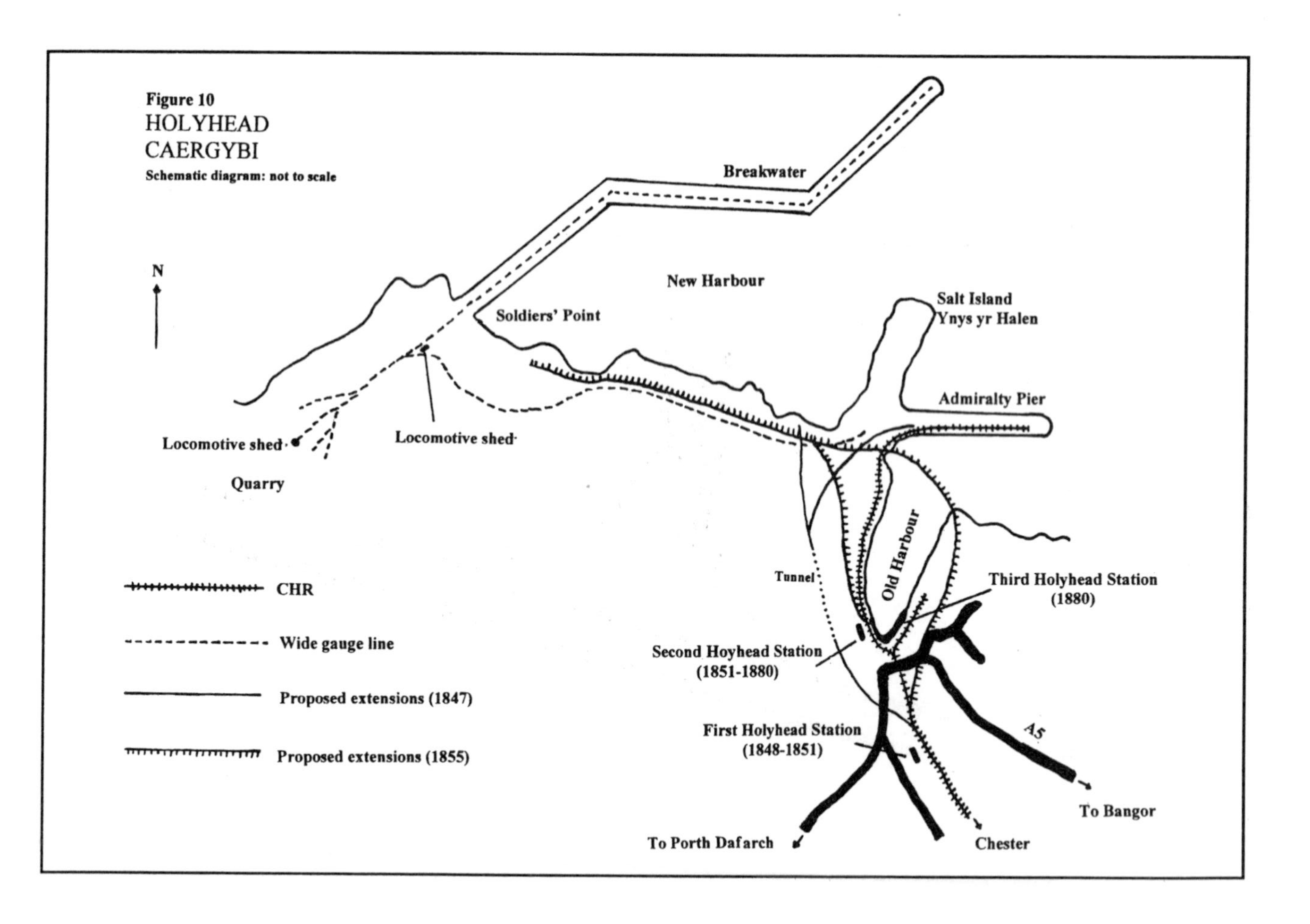

Figure 10
HOLYHEAD
CAERGYBI
Schematic diagram: not to scale
Breakwater
N
New Harbour
Soldiers' Point
Salt Island
Ynys yr Halen
Admiralty Pier
Locomotive shed
Locomotive shed
Quarry
Old Harbour
Tunnel
Third Holyhead Station
(1880)
CHR
Wide gauge line
Proposed extensions (1847)
Proposed extensions (1855)
Second Hoyhead Station
(1851-1880)
First Holyhead Station
(1848-1851)
A5
To Bangor
To Porth Dafarch
Chester

A Bill of 1855 empowered the CHR to build two extensions meeting at the South Shore and proceeding towards the west end of Newry Beach. These proposals were never implemented. By 1866 the quay on the west side of the harbour was completed with a large goods shed. This area of the quay was also used by passengers bound for Ireland. The east side of the harbour was further developed in the 1870s.

Extensive alterations to the railway harbour were completed in 1880, and a new station building and a hotel were opened. The station had a glass and iron roof in the style of large city stations. The new harbour, station and hotel were officially opened by the Prince of Wales (later King Edward VII) on 17 June 1880. The station was lit by electricity for the first time in 1895. In the past, several signal boxes controlled the train movements at Holyhead station; in later years, however, one large box and two ground frames controlled all movements.

Considerable investment in a container terminal occurred in the late 1960s, and improved facilities for car ferries were installed in the mid-1970s. The hotel and most of the old station was demolished to make way for new facilities in 1979, and for most of the 1980s the station was a mixture of permanent and temporary buildings. The locomotive yard was closed and the old steam shed pulled down in 1989. New railway buildings were completed in 1991, including a footbridge to connect the station with the town.

BRITANNIA BRIDGE FIRE

On the night of Saturday 23 May 1970, Stephenson's Britannia bridge was destroyed by fire. Some boys had entered the tubes to look for birds' nests and had used lighted newspapers to see their way in the dark. Unfortunately a fire started, and in a short time it became a blaze that was so fierce that the wrought iron tubes became distorted. Locals were astonished that a bridge apparently constructed of stone and wrought iron could burn so easily. Locals were largely unaware of the canopy over the tubes even though this had been in place for about 100 years. The canopy contained bitumen and, in addition, the rails themselves were supported on timbers within the tubes. The bridge therefore contained considerable quantities of combustible material. Consequently, once the fire had taken hold there was plenty of fuel to sustain it. Firemen were hampered in their efforts by difficulties of access to the bridge. The wrought iron tubes were severely damaged and began to sag and split under their own weight.

A decision concerning the future of the bridge had to be made as a matter of urgency. A container service to the Irish Republic had commenced in January 1968, and by the time of the fire a considerable investment had been made in a new container terminal at Holyhead. In addition a considerable volume of business came from the direction of the then newly established Rio Tinto Zinc (Anglesey Aluminium) at Holyhead, the Wylfa Nuclear Power Station as well as the Octel Company at Amlwch. There was also a considerable volume of passenger traffic to and from Holyhead. These factors made it absolutely essential to reopen the bridge. Within days the decision to reconstruct the bridge had been taken.

The Octel company had relied on railway transport since it was established at Amlwch in the early 1950s. Sulphur was brought by rail from Mostyn Docks in Flintshire, but after the fire the sulphur was brought ashore at Holyhead and conveyed by rail to Amlwch. The wagons used were actually brought to Anglesey by being winched across the damaged Britannia bridge.

Since the bridge was clearly going to be unusable for some considerable time, some locomotives and rolling stock were removed from Anglesey by road and by sea. The bridge was extensively rebuilt, but without the familiar tubes which had made it such a familiar landmark. It was decided to retain Francis Thompson's original stone towers but to build a new steel arched structure to support the railway. The new bridge was designed by Husband and Company, and the contractors were the Cleveland Bridge and Engineering Company Ltd of Darlington.

The new steel arches were completed towards the end of 1971 and trains began to run across the bridge on 30 January 1972. At this stage Stephenson's tubes were still in place but supported by the arches. The Up line was used for traffic from both directions, so that all trains passed through the Up tube. The Down tube could now be gradually demolished; pieces were carried to the mainland where they were broken up. By November 1973 the Down tube had disappeared and had been replaced by a deck. Track was then laid on this Down side (which became the permanent Up and Down routes) and all traffic was transferred to it on 2 December 1973. The Up tube could then be demolished and removed; by May 1974 this work was complete. The work did not finally end until early in 1975. Sadly, this work cost lives: on the memorial erected in Llanfair Pwllgwyngyll churchyard to remember those who died building the original Britannia bridge, two further names are inscribed.

The familiar stone lions (two on each side of the bridge) are not visible to motorists using the bridge. They can be seen below the road deck (at railway level) on both sides of the bridge. Nearby (on the mainland side of the Straits) can also be seen a small section of Stephenson's original tube.

Work on an upper road deck on the Britannia bridge was started in October 1977, and was completed in July 1980. The bridge was officially opened by HRH The Prince of Wales on 11 July 1980.

Chapter 3
THE ANGLESEY CENTRAL RAILWAY

One of the major criticisms of the Chester and Holyhead Railway was that it provided a very poor service to Anglesey residents. It did not serve the more populated areas (apart from Holyhead), and most of its stations were in sparsely-populated rural areas in the south of the island. It was, in essence, a service to connect England with Ireland, and did not have the intention of providing a comprehensive local service for Anglesey.

It was reported that as early as 1852, officials of the Chester and Holyhead Railway had surveyed in the Llangefni area with a view to providing a branch line. However, this plan did not come to fruition.

In the 1850s, the provision of single track branch lines off the main lines was proving to be big business. Such services were mushrooming all over Britain. It was William Dew, a Llangefni man and a successful estate agent, who is credited with actively pursuing the idea for a branch line to serve central parts of Anglesey. Part of the original plan was that the proposed railway could carry mineral resources from the Mynydd Parys area in order to increase the line's income, even though, at this time, activity at Mynydd Parys had been in decline for some time (and would virtually come to a halt in the 1870s). A plan was presented at a meeting in Llangefni on 5 July 1861. The main speaker was William Dew, and the meeting was chaired by Sir Richard Bulkeley. The cost of the venture was estimated as £150,000. The intention was that the railway should run from the main line at Gaerwen, through Llangefni, Llannerch-y-medd and on to Porth Amlwch, the total distance being 18½ miles. From there it was envisaged that the railway should continue towards Cemaes, through Llanrhuddlad before joining the main line at Valley. It was estimated that the building costs, including the stations, for the Gaerwen to Porth Amlwch section would be £7,000 per mile. In a meeting in Llangefni in August 1861, David Davies (of Llandinam) offered to build the railway for £6,000 per mile, provided the Company bought the land. David Davies had been involved in the construction of other railways, such as the Llanidloes and Newtown Railway and the Vale of Clwyd Railway. Davies' offer was not taken up. Various approaches were made to the LNWR in 1862 concerning the building of a line between Gaerwen and Amlwch, but the LNWR expressed no interest in such a scheme.

In the beginning, this was very much an Anglesey-based enterprise. Its intention was to serve the needs of local people, which the Chester and Holyhead Railway had failed to do. Unfortunately, the people of Anglesey were reluctant to delve deeply into their pockets to fund the project. Perhaps the financial problems encountered by the Chester and Holyhead Railway were fresh in their memories, and they feared that this new venture would suffer the same fate. However, rich landowners Lord and Lady Dinorben gave land in exchange for shares, and Sir Richard Bulkeley gave an acre of land in Llangefni for use as a station. In 1863, the contractors Dickson and Russell of Neath received £100,000 in shares so that work could begin. It was not altogether unusual for contractors to have a stake in small branch lines at this time. The Neath and Brecon Railway (who had some connection with the contractors) had three of their directors on the board of the Anglesey Railway Company, and it is certain that they, too, had some financial say in the proceedings.

The Bill permitting the construction of the line was passed by Parliament on 13 July 1863; this Bill permitted the construction of a line from Gaerwen station to the Port of Amlwch. Finally, the Central Anglesey Railway Company were in business! The official ceremony to cut the first sod took place on 11 September 1863. This ceremony was performed by Mrs W. Bulkeley Hughes (whose husband was, by then, one of the main supporters of the venture) on common land close to the proposed location of the track near the Parish Church at Llangefni. According to press reports, Mrs Hughes was presented with a small wooden wheelbarrow to mark the occasion, and there was a procession of shareholders, dignitaries and schoolchildren through the streets of Llangefni. However, work on the new line did not begin until 1864. The project engineer was a Mr Colin MacKenzie and the director a Mr McKim, both Scotsmen. Local Welsh workers formed the bulk of the labour force; they were generally praised for their conduct.

By October 1864, the single line track was almost complete from Gaerwen to Llangefni, although, by then, the path of the line between these two stations was slightly more westerly than the original 1863 Bill allowed (this deviation had been sanctioned by the authorities). The LNWR (who by then owned the Chester and Holyhead Railway) were authorised to make the connection at Gaerwen (at the Central Anglesey Line's expense). The LNWR also formed an agreement with the Central Anglesey Railway for the use of Gaerwen station and the provision of some stock.

The first train left Bangor for Llangefni on 16 December 1864 with company directors and local dignitaries on board and made the journey to a temporary station at Llangefni (about a quarter of a mile south of the permanent station). About 100 guests were entertained by the contractors at the Bull Hotel, Llangefni followed by further refreshments in the British Hotel Bangor in the afternoon. A freight service began on the line about two weeks later. The Line was inspected by the Board of Trade in February and March 1865, and on 8 March 1865 it was opened to passenger traffic. During the six-month period ending on 31 December 1865, the 4½-mile section between Gaerwen and Llangefni was used by almost 19,000 passengers and nearly 4000 tons of merchandise had been carried.

Constructing the remainder of the line continued, but money was getting short and more capital needed to be raised. The company was in a dire financial situation at this time. One of the contractors, Russell, asked the LNWR to adopt the line in August 1865, and in November of the same year the Anglesey Central Railway were seeking powers to lease or sell to the LNWR or to Russell's partner John Dickson. At the same time a 4.24 mile (6.78

km) branch from Rhos-goch to Cemaes was being considered, with a terminus near Cemaes harbour (Grid Reference SH 370 936). The route was surveyed and plans drawn, but the branch was never built. Nevertheless a further 6½ miles of track was completed to reach Llannerch-y-medd. The station was built at Brynygwalciau from where stone for its construction was obtained. This section of the line was inspected by Captain Rich, the Board of Trade Inspector. According to press reports, the Captain was very impressed by the line's construction and it opened for public use on Thursday 1 February 1866. The first train made the journey from Gaerwen to Llannerch-y-medd in 30 minutes. By that time a permanent station had been built in Llangefni, and sidings installed. There was one station between Llangefni and Llannerch-y-medd, at Llangwyllog; this station was opened in April 1866. There were four trains per day.

The Anglesey Central Railway Act of 1866 allowed the company to make arrangements with the LNWR for lease or sale, or with the contractor Dickson for lease or working. In the same year, the LNWR offered to work the Anglesey Central Railway for 60% of the gross profits. The Anglesey Central Railway company had virtually no money and they owed £40,000 to 'debenture holders' and £12,000 in loans.

The final 6¾ miles to the terminus at Amlwch (see Appendix) was also a single track with one intermediate station at Rhos-goch. It was opened to passenger traffic on 1 June 1867, although it seems that the line had been used for freight traffic for a few months prior to this. In fact, advertisements placed by the Anglesey Central Railway in the local press stated that the line was open to Amlwch for 'merchandise traffic' from March 1867.

As an indication of the fares in 1867, a third class single ticket from Gaerwen to Llangefni cost 0s.4½d. (2 pence), to Llannerch-y-medd 0s.11d. (4½ pence) and to Amlwch 1s.5½d. (7½ pence).

The Anglesey Central Line had never enjoyed a sound financial footing and had always been short of money. This is shown by the involvement of other companies and contractors in its affairs. It was too weak financially to buy its own locomotives and rolling stock and had to resort to hiring them from the rich LNWR company and this was financially crippling. This arrangement continued until early 1876 when Anglesey Central Railway was unable to reach agreement concerning the supply of locomotives and rolling stock with the LNWR. Later in the same year (1 July 1876), the Anglesey Central Line was sold to the LNWR for £80,000 (less than its initial building costs). The entire history of the line had been a financial disaster; now the rich LNWR was taking advantage of the hard work of the Anglesey people and acquiring a branch line at a bargain price.

The LNWR found that the track was, in places, in a poor state, and the stations were dirty and required upgrading. The bridges and fences also required some work. Consequently, the new company carried out a number of improvements over the next few years. This upgrading work could never have been carried out by the Anglesey Railway Company. A passing loop was installed in Llangefni in 1877, and a siding in Llannerch-y-medd. A locomotive shed and sidings were built at Amlwch in 1878. New station buildings were erected at Pentreberw, Llangwyllog and Rhos-goch in 1882, and improvements to station buildings at Amlwch in 1884. Platform extensions were completed at Llangefni in 1887 and at Pentreberw, Rhos-goch and Llangwyllog in 1890. Much later, in 1914, a passing loop was provided at Llangwyllog, together with an Up platform. The Amlwch line was never provided with turntables (see Appendix) to turn locomotives around and provide for more flexible working. It also had no signal boxes.

When Britain's Railways were rationalised in 1923, the LNWR was absorbed into the LMSR (see Appendix). The period between the First World War and the 1930s was a time of declining traffic and cutbacks in order to save money. The Amlwch locomotive shed was closed on 14 September 1930, and the work was transferred to Bangor. The shed was later demolished.

In 1952, a private extension to the line was opened at Amlwch to connect the line to the Associated Ethyl Company (also known as the Octel Company) at Porth Amlwch. This extension was to be used to carry chemicals in rail-tankers to and from the plant. The Octel Company extracted bromine from sea water at Amlwch. The chlorine required for the process was transported into the plant in tankers, and ethylene dibromide was carried out. Ethylene dibromide was used in the petrochemicals industry to manufacture an antiknock ingredient for petrol (leaded petrol). Sulphur was also transported from Mostyn Docks in Flintshire to the Octel works by rail. In 1984, Octel entered into an agreement with the rail authorities to keep the line open and well-maintained into the 1990s. This arrangement continued until about 1994 when the company decided that it would be more economic to transport these chemicals by road. Sadly, this marked the beginning of the line's decline into its present state.

In the 1970s, a private siding (junction at Grid Reference SH 419 907) was constructed off the line between Rhos-goch and Amlwch to the Shell Tank Farm (Grid Reference SH 410 906). The junction is 1.0 miles (1.6 km) north of Rhos-goch. The tank farm stored crude oil which had come ashore from large tankers at the Shell Marine Terminal near Amlwch. The oil was pumped from the tank farm by pipeline all the way to the Shell refinery at Stanlow in Cheshire. This was a major engineering project; however, it had a very short life, and after its closure the site was cleared. The site is now in the hands of Anglesey County Council, but the railway siding is still in place.

In Autumn 1877, there was a spell of heavy rain which led to a serious accident on the Anglesey Central Line. About 1.4 miles (2.2 km) north of Llannerch-y-medd the river Alaw flows parallel to the railway line for a short distance after which the line crosses the river over a stone bridge (not far from Cae Mawr, Grid Reference SH 418 850). Unfortunately, on the night of 29 November 1877, this bridge was washed away. This was caused by a torrent of water which was released when the dam at Pandy lake was ruptured by the weight of water. The following morning, shortly after 6 a.m., the first train of the day steamed by in the darkness, the locomotive and most of the carriages fell into the swollen river below. It was a scene of utter devastation. Fortunately, there was only one passenger on the train. Sadly, three men were badly burned by hot steam and died within hours despite receiving help at the scene from a local doctor. One of those killed was a Mr John Davies of Gaerwen, who had been an inspector on the Anglesey

Central Line for some years. It is said to have taken some time to clear the area of debris and rebuild the bridge so that the service could continue.

Another tragic accident occurred at Llannerch-y-medd on the night of Friday 10 December 1926. The driver of a train from Gaerwen to Amlwch reported that the train had struck an obstacle just outside Llannerch-y-medd at 9:52 p.m. A search of the track followed and the bodies of a 27-year old man and a 23-year old woman were discovered. Both were local and were in service at a nearby farm. An inquest reported an open verdict.

The Gaerwen to Amlwch line finally closed on 7 December 1964. This came about as a result of the Beeching Report of 1963 (see Appendix). This report blamed the losses of British Railways on rising costs, fewer passengers and declining freight traffic. Thus ended a period of Anglesey history, the line having served generations of Anglesey people and businesses for almost exactly 100 years.

Ten years or so later, Anglesey County Council explored the possibility of re-opening the line to passenger services, but the plan did not come to fruition. Some years later, in 1991, Isle of Anglesey Railways Ltd was set up. Its establishment was the result of a public meeting to gauge the extent of public support for the re-opening the whole of the line from Amlwch to Gaerwen. Interest was shown by the public as well as public bodies such as Gwynedd County Council, the then Ynys Môn Borough Council, the Wales Tourist Board and the Welsh Development Agency.

Following a feasibility study, negotiation took place between Isle of Anglesey Railways and Railtrack, the owners of the line, as well as a number of other bodies, regarding its possible purchase. In May and August 1992 special passenger trains (organised by Isle of Anglesey Railways Ltd.) ran on the line using Diesel Multiple Units and the last passenger excursion was in 1994. In 1999, it was reported that discussions with Ynys Môn County Council (the new unitary authority established in 1996) were still proceeding. Later the same year, the local press reported that maintenance work was being carried out along the whole length of the line by volunteers. Despite objections from freight operator

*The Britannia Bridge showing the steel arches added after the 1970 fire.
Here the road deck is in the process of being added. (July 1979)*

Section of Stephenson's Tubular Bridge on the mainland side of the Menai Straits, showing the cellular construction at the top and bottom (July 2004)

*Train leaving
Llanfair Pwllgwyngyll station
(August 2004)*

Llanfair Pwllgwyngyll Station showing the unused station building and footbridge. (July 2004)

Llanfair Pwllgwyngyll

Llanfair Pwllgwyngyll station (November 2004)

Train approaching Llanfair Pwllgwyngyll station (August 2004)

Gaerwen, viewed from the level crossing and looking towards Holyhead. The signalbox is on the right. Note the crossover which is still in place. The connection to the Amlwch line can be seen in the distance. (July 2004)

Bodorgan Station (August 2004)

Bodorgan station, looking towards Bangor. (August 2004)

Bodorgan Station, looking towards Holyhead. Note the steps on the Up platform. This is because this platform is lower than the Down platform. (July 2004)

Train approaching Bodorgan Tunnels (August 2004)

Train leaving Bodorgan station (August 2004)

The Bodorgan tunnels looking towards Bodorgan Station. The longest tunnel is in the foreground. (July 2004)

Train stopped at Bodorgan station (August 2004)

Diesel Locomotive at Holyhead station (August 2004)

Tŷ Croes Station showing level crossing and signal-box. The Down platform is on the right, and the Up platform is beyond the level crossing (July 2004)

Valley Station showing the level crossing and the signalbox. Beyond the level crossing a branch curves towards the Valley sidings (July 2004)

Holyhead Station (August 2004)

Holyhead Station (August 2004)

Holyhead Station looking towards Valley (August 2004)

Pentreberw: Anglesey Central Line passes under the new A55 where new track and ballast were laid. In the foreground the track is overgrown.

Near Llangefni Station: Anglesey Central Line passes over bridge near path through Nant y Pandy. Station building is hidden by trees in the distance (July 2004)

The Anglesey Central Line passing through open countryside near Ynys Llyn (SH 417805) between Llangwyllog and Llannerch-y-medd. Note the better condition of the track in this area (July 2004)

Llannerch-y-medd Station showing the surviving station building and platform. The former stationmaster's house is in the background on the right. (July 2004)

Llannerch-y-medd Station showing its overgrown state. The roof of the station building can be seen on the left as well as the edge of the platform. The track can be seen in the distance. (July 2004)

Llannerch-y-medd Station with former goods yard used as car park. Station building is on left and Stationmaster's house is the highest house in the background (July 2004)

Amlwch – near site of former station. The track leads to the former Great Lakes (Octel) site about 0.5 mile (0.8 km) away. Note the lever to operate the points for the loop and the sign warning of a level crossing. (July 2004)

Red Wharf Bay and Benllech line – construction work (circa. 1907).

Pentreberw station (then known officially as Holland Arms) showing the first train to Pentraeth (1 July 1908)

Pentre Berw station (then known officially as Holland Arms) showing a group of mostly children on the platform (and the track) on the opening day of the line to Pentraeth (1 July 1908)

Ceint station looking towards Rhyd y Saint, with a motor train in the distance.

Rhyd y Saint station, looking towards Pentraeth (circa 1908)

Pentraeth Station. Note the exposed location of the station (1909)

Pentraeth Station, showing the rudimentary station buildings (1909)

Red Wharf Bay and Benllech station, probably during its construction. The men pictured may be Railway or construction officials (circa 1909)

Red Wharf Bay and Benllech Station (circa 1909)

Two bridges over the old Pentre Berw to Red Wharf Bay line, near Pentre Berw (August 2004)

EWS, press reports stated that Isle of Anglesey Railways were still optimistic in early 2000. Later the same year the Company were given two locomotives (a Hunslet and a Rushton) by the Great Lakes Company (formerly Octel) of Amlwch. In 2000, the original line at Pentreberw had to be lifted to allow work on the new A55, but was subsequently re-laid with new sleepers, chairs and ballast (see Appendix).

As recently as November 2000, members of Ynys Môn County Council's cabinet reaffirmed their commitment to purchase the line. At the same time, it was reported that Burlington Resources Ltd (who had expressed an interest in establishing a gas-fired power station at Rhos-goch, on the site of the old Shell Tank Farm) was interested in using the line to transport materials to Rhos-goch. By the middle of 2001, however, it seemed that the project was in some considerable doubt and that Ynys Môn County Council had apparently withdrawn its support. At the time of writing, the future of the line is uncertain, and the condition of the track is deteriorating.

LOCOMOTIVES AND ROLLING STOCK

During the construction of the Amlwch line, various locomotives had been used by the contractors Dickson and Russell. They had used Fairlie type locomotives (see Appendix) named *Progress* and *Mountaineer,* both new and built by James Cross and Company, Sutton Engine Works, St. Helens, Lancashire. Also used by the contractors was a Hawthorn 0-6-0WT well tank engine called *Anglesea* which was owned by the Neath and Brecon Railway. This latter locomotive must still have been on the line at the end of 1867 because solicitors acting for the Neath and Brecon Railway were instructed to recover it in December 1867. When services began on the line, LNWR locomotives and rolling stock were used, since the Anglesey Central Railways did not have the means to buy its own. Passenger trains used LNWR locomotives, such as the Webb designed 1P 2-4-2T tank engine (see Appendix), and freight was hauled by LNWR 0-6-0 tender locomotives. Much later, when the LMSR company owned the line, Class 27 3F 0-6-0 tender engines (of Aspinall design, see Appendix) were used for some years, mostly for passenger services.

From 1948, Ivatt (LMSR designed) Class 2MT 2-6-2T locomotives (the basis of the later BR Standard Class 2MT; see Appendix) were used and they found extensive use over the line for freight and passenger purposes. They were well-designed and very popular with drivers and firemen who had been used to the cramped conditions on the aged LNWR Webb 2-4-2T locomotives. Passenger rolling stock were usually of the non-corridor type.

In May 1953, an A.E.C. Diesel Railcar (for passenger traffic) was tested on the line; it was criticised for its rough ride but otherwise the trial proved fairly successful. Steam services resumed immediately after the trial was completed. In 1956, Derby lightweight two-coach Diesel units (DMUs) made their first appearance on the line (see Appendix). These units took over most of the passenger services, and proved to be more popular than the A.E.C. units as they gave a smoother ride.

From the late 1950s, BR Standard Class 2MT 2-6-0 tender locomotives (of Ivatt design, see Appendix) were used to haul freight trains. In the summer of 1963 and 1964, due to a shortage of DMUs, steam locomotives made a come-back on the Amlwch line. BR Standard Class 2MT 2-6-2T locomotives were used to power push-pull sets (see Appendix). The DMUs returned into service in the winter.

In 1964, British Railways Standard Class 4MT 2-6-4T locomotives (of Stanier type) and Stanier designed Class 5MT 4-6-0 tender locomotives (sometimes known as the Stanier 'Black Five' which later developed into the BR Class 5 locomotive; see Appendix) were used for freight haulage. Soon after, the line closed and only freight workings to the Octel works at Amlwch were using the line. The tank wagons were hauled to Amlwch, and Octel's own Diesel shunter locomotive took them into the plant itself. BR steam locomotives did not enter the Octel works. When Diesel locomotives were subsequently used for this work, they did enter the works.

STATIONS

Gaerwen (Grid Reference SH 485 708)
This station was opened in January 1849 and was connected to the Anglesey Central Line in 1864. For further details see Chapter 2.

Pentreberw (Grid Reference SH 471 726)
This station (Figure 11), known officially as Holland Arms was opened on 12 March 1865. It was 2¼ miles (3.6 km) from Gaerwen. It had a single platform on the Down side with a wooden building housing a waiting room and booking office. This was replaced in 1882 (by the LNWR) by a brick building similar to Rhos-goch and Llangwyllog. A goods yard handling minerals (e.g. coal) and livestock was to be found on the Down side. Pentreberw was originally an intermediate halt, but was upgraded in 1908 when the Red Wharf line began so that Gaerwen to Pentreberw became a section (see Appendix). At the same time, a new platform was constructed on the Up side to serve the Red Wharf Bay line. However, in 1925 Gaerwen to Llangefni was made a single section again. With the final closure of the Red Wharf line in 1950, traffic declined and the station was closed to all traffic on 4 August 1952. The platforms were subsequently removed; the buildings are now in private ownership. The yard is used as a coal business.

Llangefni (Grid Reference SH 456 758)
The permanent station (Figure 12) at Llangefni was opened on 26 January 1866; a previous temporary station stood about a quarter of a mile to the south (as shown by contemporary OS maps). It was 4½ miles (7.2 km) from Gaerwen. The two storey station buildings were on the Up side. There was a short loop on the Down side, but this was not used for allowing passenger trains to pass. The station had a busy goods yard, handling flour, livestock, agricultural products and coal. Signals and points were controlled from a 16 lever frame mounted on the platform, porter/signalmen being employed to do this work. The loop and the goods yard were dismantled after the station's closure in 1964.

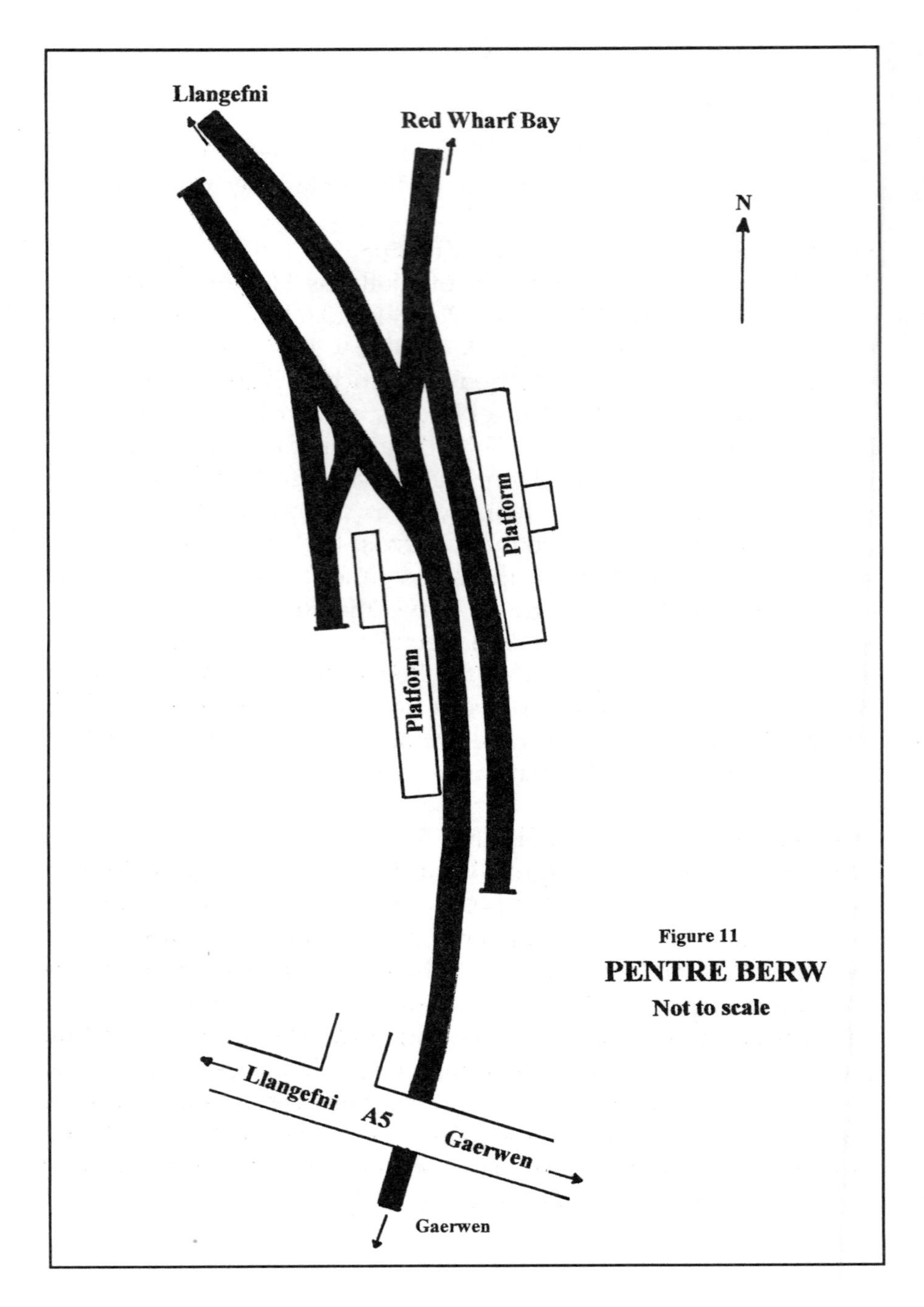

Figure 11
PENTRE BERW
Not to scale

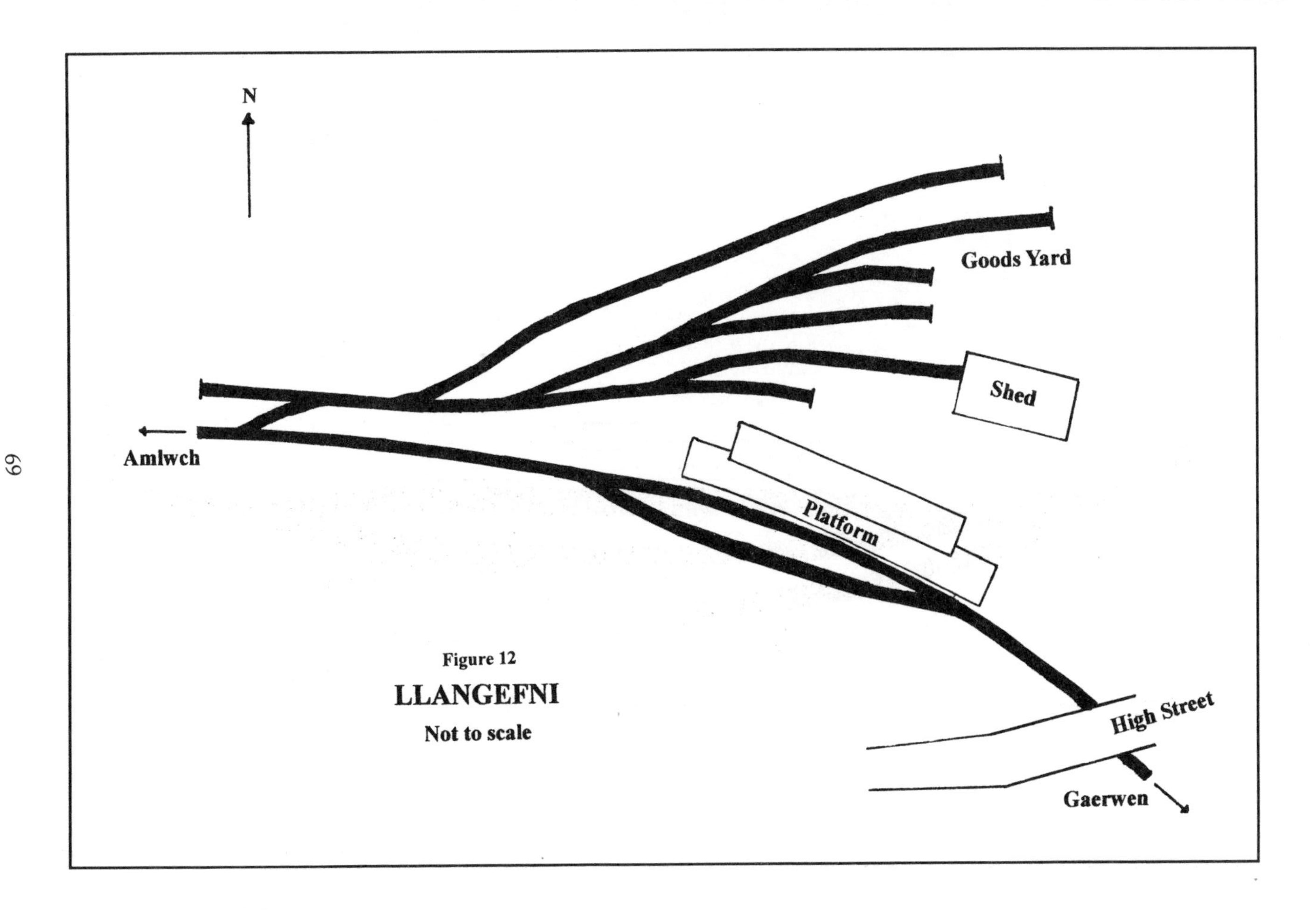

Figure 12
LLANGEFNI
Not to scale

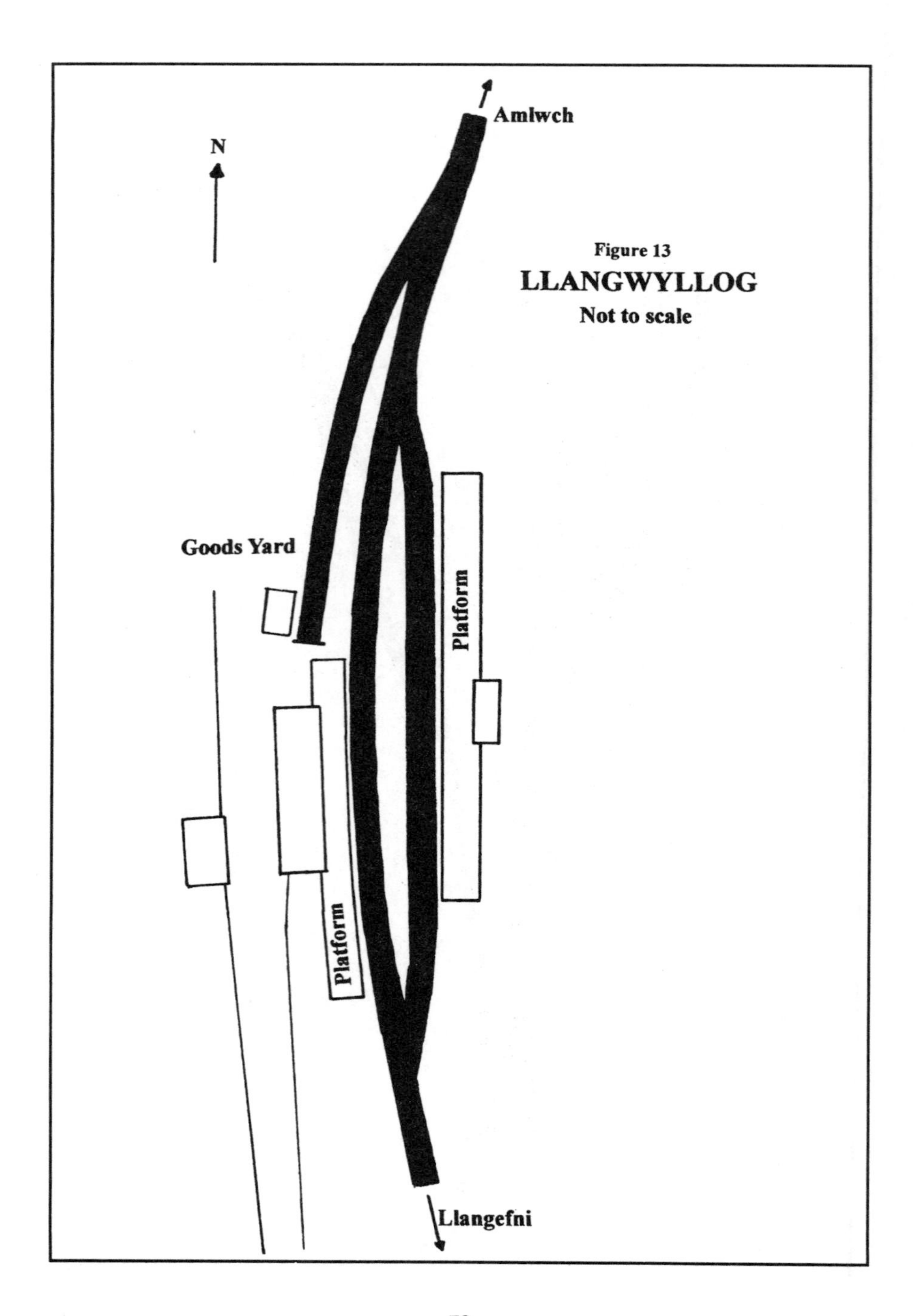
Amlwch
N
Figure 13
LLANGWYLLOG
Not to scale
Goods Yard
Platform
Platform
Llangefni

Llangwyllog (Grid Reference SH 436 790)
This station (Figure 13) was opened in April 1866, as an intermediate halt between Llangefni and Llannerch-y-medd. It was 7 miles (11.2 km) from Gaerwen. The single storey station buildings are on the Down side (building similar to Pentreberw). The Up side platform had a wooden hut. There was a goods yard (handling livestock and coal) on the Down side at the north end of the station. In 1914, a passing loop was constructed, thereby allowing two trains to pass. This was the only point on the line where passenger trains were permitted to cross. If it were not for this feature the station might have been closed many years before the line's eventual closure. The signals and points were controlled by platform-mounted levers. The station was closed in 1964; the goods tracks and the passing loop were removed.

Llannerch-y-medd (Grid Reference SH 417 840)
This station (Figure 14) was opened in 1866, and is 11 miles (17.6 km) from Gaerwen. The platform is on the Up side. On the platform stands the small single-storey station building. Opposite the platform is a rocky outcrop, giving the station a very cramped feel. There were three sidings and the goods yard handled livestock, flour, agricultural materials and coal. There was a lever frame on the platform, as well as a 2-lever ground frame. The station was closed in 1964, when the sidings were removed and all the buildings except the station itself, were demolished. The station building is now in the hands of Ynys Môn County Council. At the time of writing, there are proposals to use the site as a railway heritage centre.

Rhos-goch (Grid Reference SH 410 894)
This station (Figure 15) was completed in 1867 and was an intermediate halt on the Llannerch-y-medd to Amlwch section. It was 14½ miles (23.2 km) from Gaerwen. It had a single platform on the Down side. The original wooden building was replaced by a brick structure in 1882. There is a goods yard (with two sidings and a goods shed) at the north end of the station. In its day, it was a busy station handling cattle, sheep, wool, grain, fertilizer and

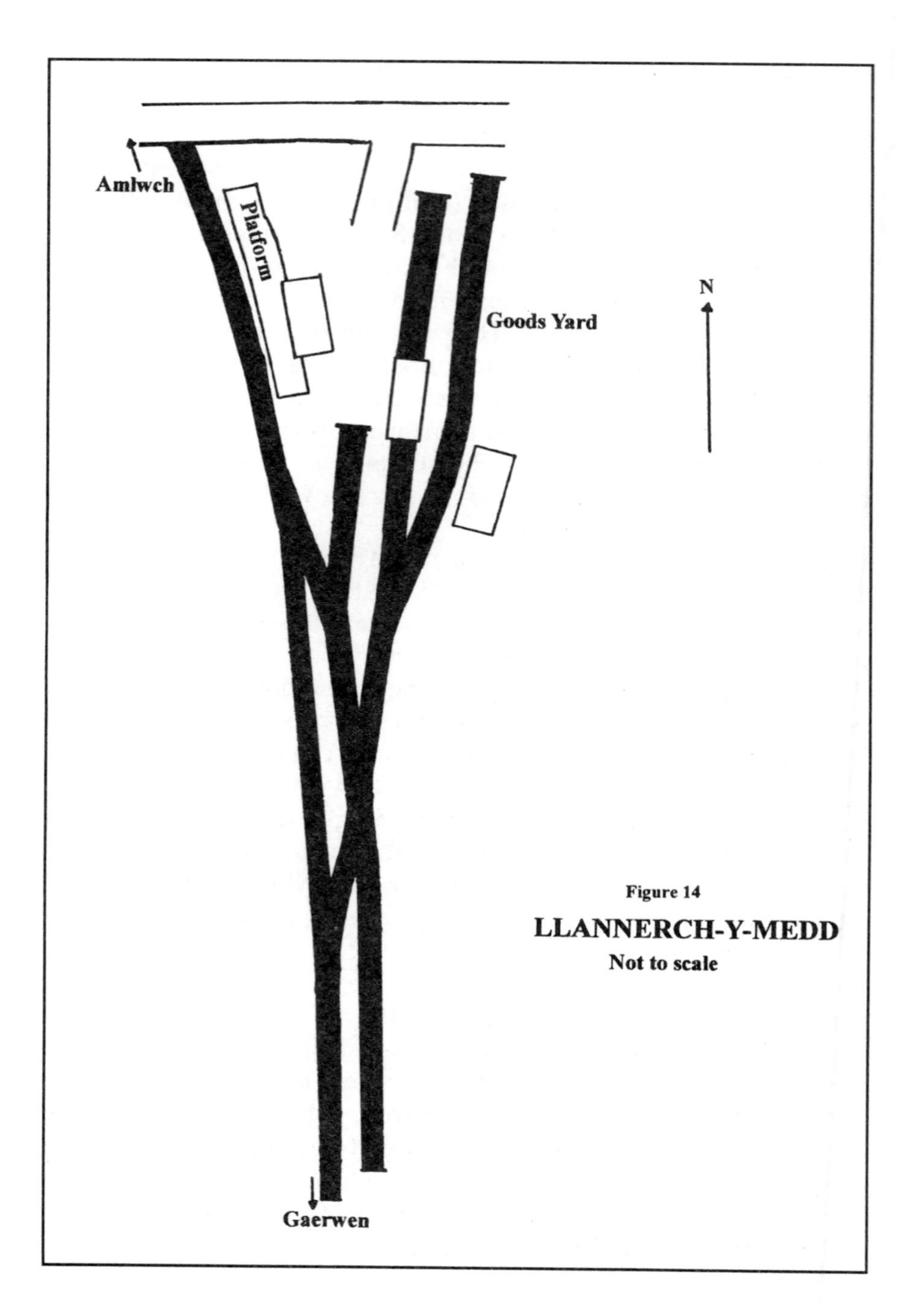

Figure 14

LLANNERCH-Y-MEDD

Not to scale

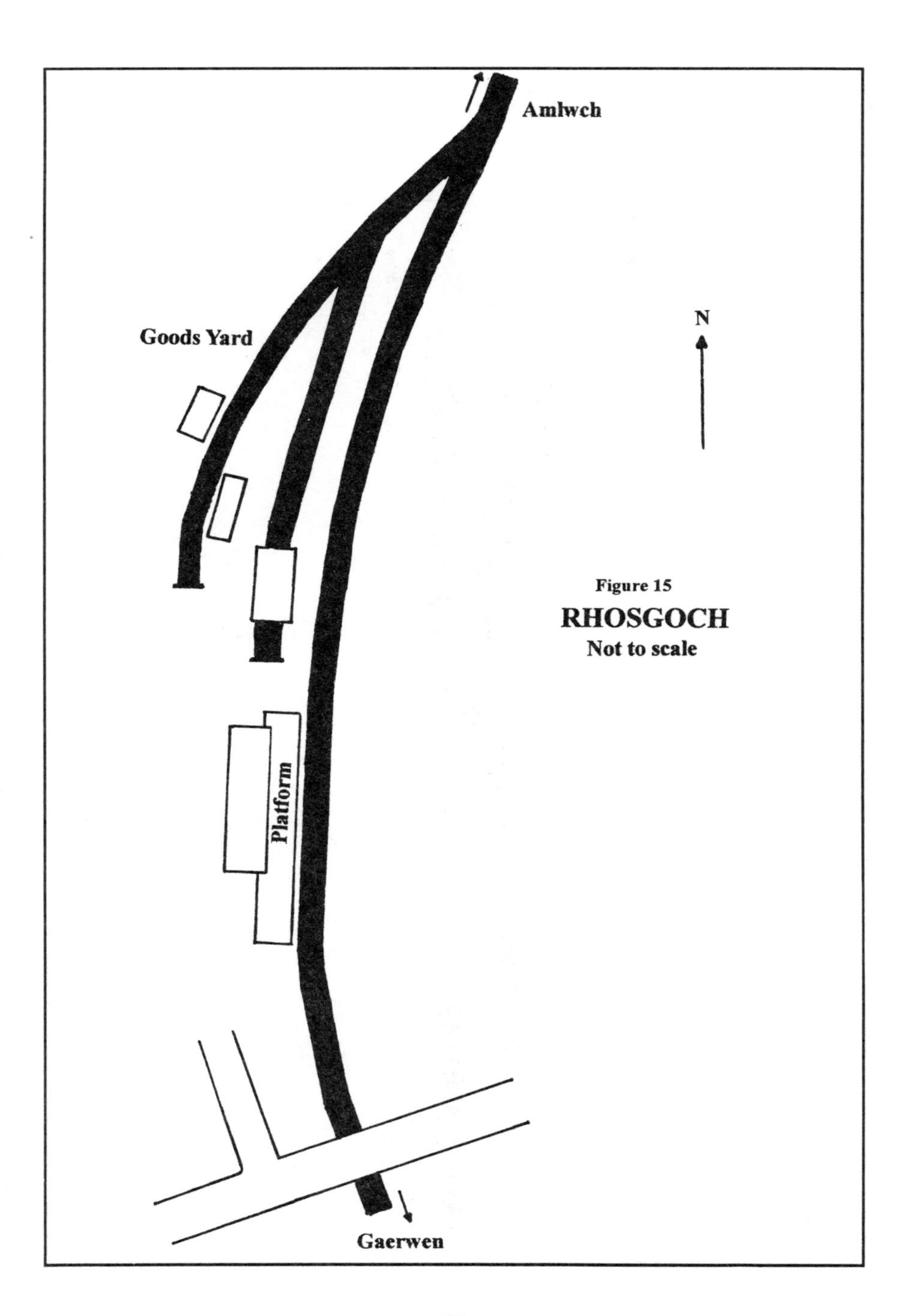

Figure 15
RHOSGOCH
Not to scale

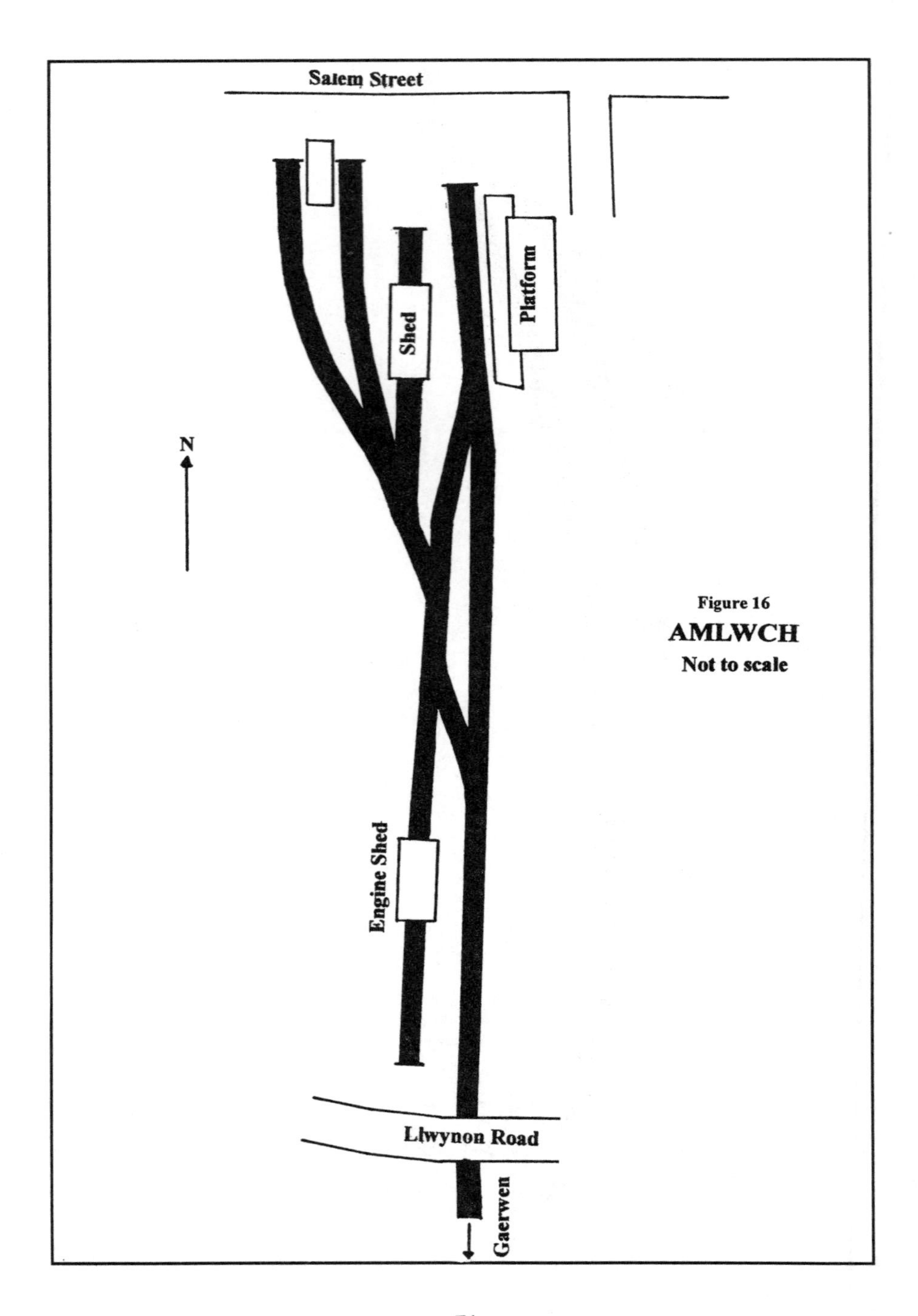

Figure 16
AMLWCH
Not to scale

coal. A two-lever ground frame controlled movements to and from the goods yard. After the station was closed in 1964, the sidings were removed and the goods shed demolished. The station building is in private ownership. In the mid-1970s a private siding was built to connect the line with the Shell Tank Farm. This site has since been cleared and is now owned by Ynys Môn County Council, but the siding is still intact.

Amlwch (Grid Reference SH 442 928)
Amlwch station (Figure 16) was officially opened in 1867. It is 17¾ miles (28.4 km) from Gaerwen and had the most extensive facilities on the line. The passenger platform was on the Up side. It had a goods yard (having three sidings) with cattle pens and a goods warehouse, handling coal, flour, raw tobacco (for the small Amlwch tobacco industry), fresh fish etc. Train crews working the Amlwch line were based at locomotive sheds at Bangor and Amlwch. The Amlwch locomotive shed (employing a total of 9 staff, including 3 drivers) was closed in 1931, and the work then transferred to the Bangor shed. A lever frame near the platform controlled the signals and points. This was originally uncovered, although a cover is said to have been built much later. In 1952, a cabin was built. The station was closed in December 1964, and the loop removed in 1984. The station building itself was demolished during the 1970s when a bypass road was built, but a brick-built shed remains, now in private hands. Freight traffic to the Octel works continued to pass through the station until 1994.

Chapter 4
THE PENTREBERW TO RED WHARF BAY LINE

In 1897, the LNWR submitted a proposal to build a new line to connect Llanfair Pwllgwyngyll to Benllech. The purpose of the line was to take advantage of the tourist trade, then beginning to take hold in the area. The original intention was to take the line to the northern end of Benllech sands. There was also a proposal for the line to run from Llangefni to Benllech. Later, the proposed route was changed to Pentreberw to Benllech. An Act of Parliament of 1 August 1899 authorised the construction of the line from Pentreberw to Red Wharf Bay (to a spot about 0.1 mile from the Ship Inn). The total length of the line was 6.66 miles (10.7 km). By 1900, the plan had changed once more: now the terminus was to be at an isolated spot about half a mile south of Benllech next to the Menai Bridge to Benllech road (A5025). In addition, the line between Pentraeth and the terminus was to take a more direct route a little further from the coast making the overall length 6.62 miles (10.6 km).

Because the LNWR were undertaking a number of expensive schemes elsewhere, work did not begin on the line until June 1907, when modifications to the track at Pentreberw permitted the work to begin. The contractor was J. Strachan and Sons of Cardiff and the engineer was Mr F.G.T. Adams. Most of the construction workers were not local and came to live in the area, some with their families, for the duration of the work. The line was designed and built as a light railway (see Appendix) with no signal boxes. A single line track was constructed and this had reached Pentraeth by June 1908; it was officially inspected on 26 June 1908. This 4¾ mile (7.6 km) section of the line was opened officially on Wednesday 1 July 1908. There were intermediate halts at Ceint and Rhyd y Saint. On this day, the first scheduled train left

Gaerwen at 9:35 a.m. carrying Lord Stalbridge (LNWR Chairman), Mr L.A.P. Warner (Manager of the Chester and North Wales region), as well as other company directors and officials. The train itself was described in press reports as being drawn by a locomotive smaller than the usual branch line locomotive, and having carriages of the 'tramcar type'. At Pentraeth, the dignitaries were welcomed by Mr John Rice Roberts (Chairman of the Parish Council) and the Rev. E.P. Howells (Rector of Pentraeth). Later a sports event for children of Pentraeth, Llanbedr-goch and Tynygongl schools was held in a park opposite the Rectory, and tea for 400 people was arranged in Pentraeth school. In the evening, sports for adults were held in the park.

The final phase of the project, the 2 mile (3.2 km) section from Pentraeth to the terminus at Red Wharf Bay was opened on Monday, 24 May 1909 having been officially inspected four days earlier. The terminus was officially known as Red Wharf Bay and Benllech. There was an intermediate halt at Llanbedr-goch. The whole line was a single track, with no passing loops at any point along its length. There were, however, sidings at the Red Wharf terminus, and also at Pentraeth. At the start, there were five passenger trains each way on weekdays with six on Thursdays; there was one goods train a day. The line also provided a service to Llangefni, since trains arriving at the Pentreberw station moved onto the Amlwch line. Since Llangefni was a busy market town, this was a useful service. Passenger and freight services ran six days a week.

The opening day of the completed line on 24 May 1909 was also marked by great celebration. Mr L.A.P. Warner made another appearance and, accompanied by 20 invited guests, travelled on the first train to Benllech. Mr John Rice Roberts thanked the company who had built the line and expressed the hope that it would profitable for the LNWR and for the area. He expressed the view that Benllech could compete for tourists with areas like Llandudno. Later, a large motor car took Mr and Mrs Warner on a trip around the local area including the site of the Royal Charter disaster, Llugwy and Mynydd Parys. This was followed by a banquet for the company's officials at the Dinorben Arms Hotel in

Amlwch. The local people were not treated so generously: they had to pay 2d. for the privilege of attending a sports day for local children where bara brith was served and the Clio brass band provided entertainment. Newspaper reports suggest that hundreds of people were present.

Keziah Ellen Lewis of Tanyfron, Mynydd Llwydiarth, near Pentraeth was 11 at the time of the line's opening. Writing in the 1970s, she recalled: 'On the day of the official opening most of us children had the opportunity to travel by train for the very first time. A procession of schoolchildren marched to the station to meet the train which had already picked up children from the Tynygongl (Benllech) and Llanbedr-goch areas. We got on the train and it travelled in the direction of Rhyd y Saint. It was such a strange feeling to see the trees and hedges move past. After reaching the end of the journey, the train started its journey back to Benllech. There another procession involving the children of all three schools marched to Bryn Tirion [Hotel] where a tea party had been prepared for us. Later we played games on the lawn, and we returned home very tired that night.'

During the construction of the Red Wharf Bay line, an ancient burial site was discovered on land at Merddyn Gwyn, just outside Pentraeth on the way towards Llanbedr-goch. The then Rector of Llansadwrn, the Rev. Evan Evans took the responsibility of removing the bones. The Rev. Evans was said to be an expert in different forms of burial. He used to take some of these skeletons with him when he lectured in different locations in the area. The skeletons were displayed in a sitting position with crockery containing food and drink placed around them.

This line was the last constructed in Anglesey, and was also the last standard gauge railway to be constructed in north Wales. Unfortunately, its opening came at a time of great increase in road traffic, and the anticipated level of passenger rail traffic never materialised. Shortly after the First World War, the Anglesey area, in common with most others, saw a significant increase in the provision of bus services. This further contributed to the line's decline. Another contributory factor was, undoubtedly, the fact that the line ran through a very thinly populated part of Anglesey and that the stations were not conveniently located. Sadly, therefore, Mr John Rice Roberts' hopes were not realised.

Regular passenger services stopped on 22 September 1930, although occasional Saturday passenger services continued until 1939. These services were apparently run in conjunction with the Crosville Motor Bus Company, and were run because of delays experienced by buses on the Menai Suspension Bridge (due to weight restrictions) in the days before its reconstruction around 1940. After the War, passenger services had completely stopped, and the Menai Suspension Bridge was by then well able to cope with any type of bus. Tolls on the Menai Suspension Bridge were also abolished in 1940.

Freight services on the Red Wharf Line continued on a daily basis until 1944, when the service was reduced to three days a week. The closure of the line was considered in 1947, but it was kept open with a speed restriction of 15 mph over its entire length and the power of the locomotives used limited to class 2F (see Appendix). In post-war Britain, petrol rationing was still in place, and this may have been a consideration in keeping the line open at this stage. The line finally closed to all traffic on 3 April 1950. The track was sold to a Scottish company called James N. Campbell Ltd (of Coatbridge, near Glasgow); the track and equipment were removed between April and October 1953. As a result of the closure of the Red Wharf Bay line, there seemed to be little purpose in keeping the Pentreberw station open, and it was also closed in 1952.

LOCOMOTIVES AND ROLLING STOCK

From the start this light railway was served by push-pull sets (or Motor Trains), initially using Webb designed 2-4-0T locomotives (see Appendix). The LNWR converted two coaches for this purpose. Later 2-4-2T locomotives were used. Normally, a locomotive and two coaches would be used with one door being used because some of the line's platforms were very short (in some cases only 60ft).

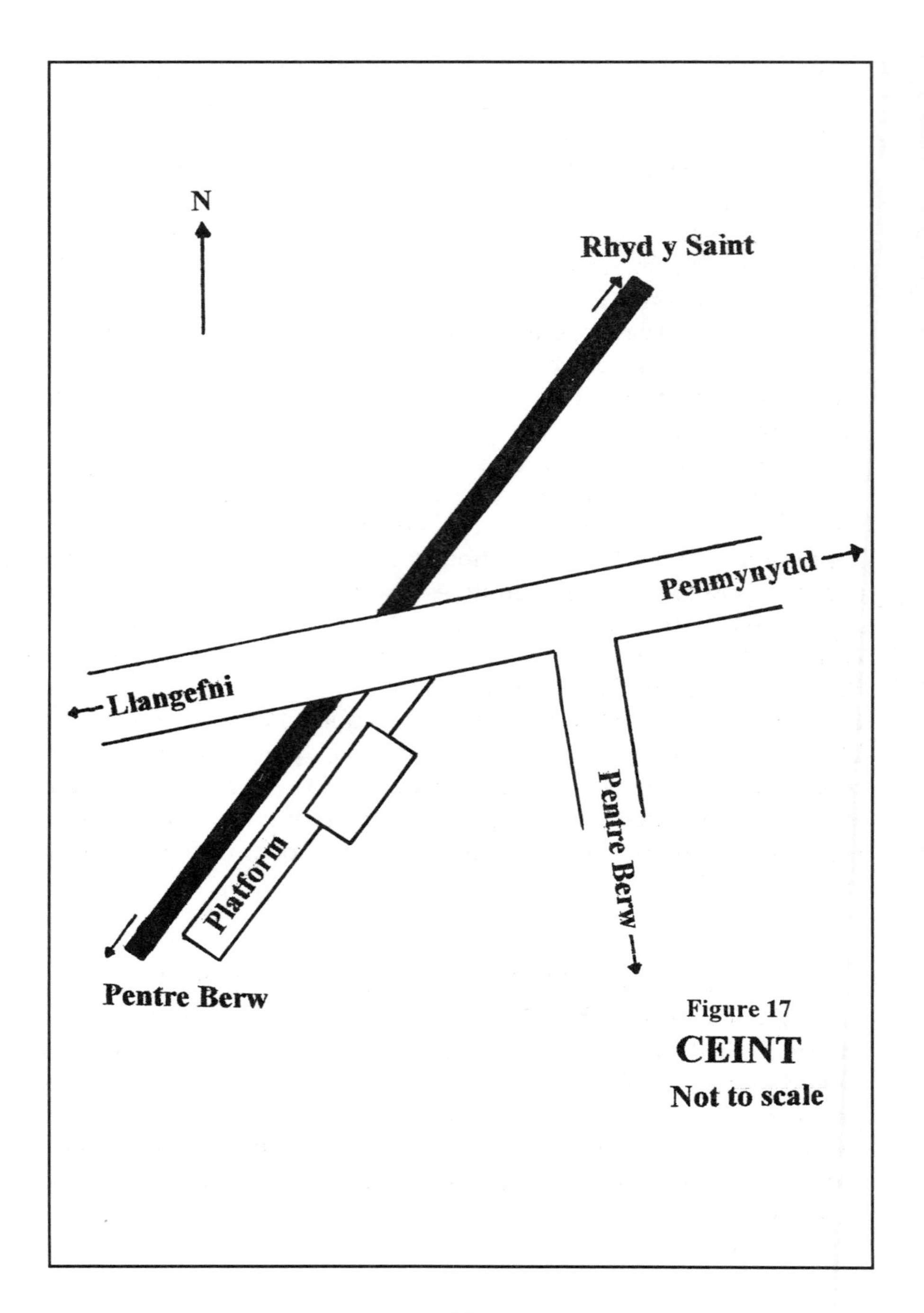

Figure 17
CEINT
Not to scale

STATIONS

Pentreberw (Grid Reference SH 471 726)
This station, known officially as Holland Arms, was opened as part of the Central Anglesey Line in March 1865. In 1907, a branch was opened up in order that construction of the Red Wharf Bay line could begin. A new platform (on the Up side) was built for this purpose.

Ceint (Grid Reference SH 488 748)
Ceint station (or more accurately, Ceint halt) was opened in 1908. It was located 1¾ miles (2.8 km) from Pentreberw. The platform (only 60 feet long) was built on the Up side with a LNWR wooden hut and name board (Figure 17). The station was unstaffed, tickets being issued by the train guard. The station was described as a *conditional halt*, which means that a train would only stop there if requested. There was no goods yard. In 1930, following the suspension of regular passenger services, the station building was removed.

Rhyd y Saint (Grid Reference SH 499 758)
Rhyd y Saint station (or halt) was opened in 1908. It was 2¾ miles (4.4 km) from Pentreberw. It is a conditional halt with a platform (60 feet long), wooden hut and name board on the Down side (Figure 18). It was unstaffed. Access to the station was by steps from the minor road passing over the line. There was no goods yard. The station closed in 1930 and the site was cleared. The name Rhyd y Saint denotes the ford where Afon Ceint crosses the old Post Road from Beaumaris. The origin of the name Rhyd y Saint (Ford of the Saints) is not entirely clear. Perhaps it derives its name from the path taken by the faithful who attended the nearby Llanffinan Church, or it describes the meeting point of St. Seiriol and St. Cybi.

Pentraeth (Grid Reference SH 518 753)
This was one of the two largest stations on the line and is 4¾ miles (7.6 km) from Pentreberw. It was opened on 1 July 1908, and

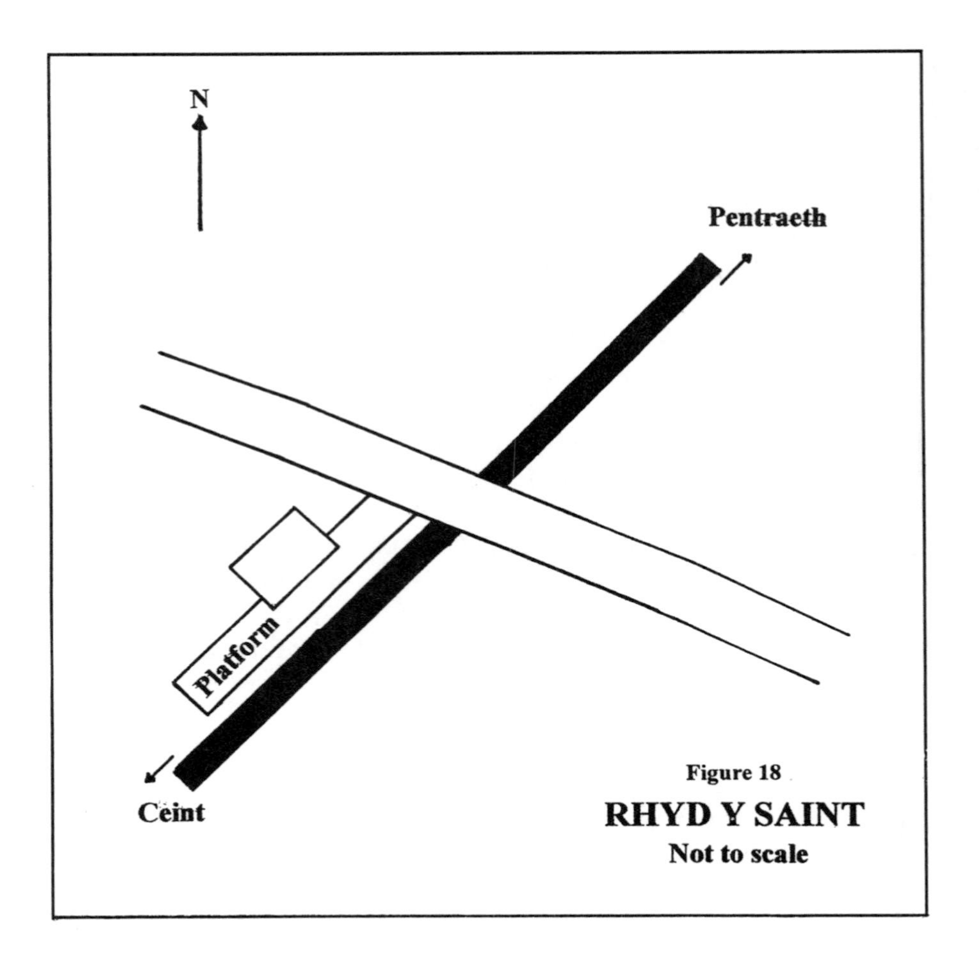

Figure 18
RHYD Y SAINT
Not to scale

stands about a quarter of a mile from the centre of the village in a fairly exposed position (Figure 19). It had a 120 ft. platform and a small cluster of huts on the Up side of the line. It had a small goods yard, a warehouse, a cattle pen, facilities for handling coal and was permanently staffed (although the maximum number employed here was two). A ground frame controlled movements to and from the sidings. The station closed in 1950 after all traffic ceased. A bridge over the nearby Pentraeth to Talwrn road was removed sometime in the 1960s.

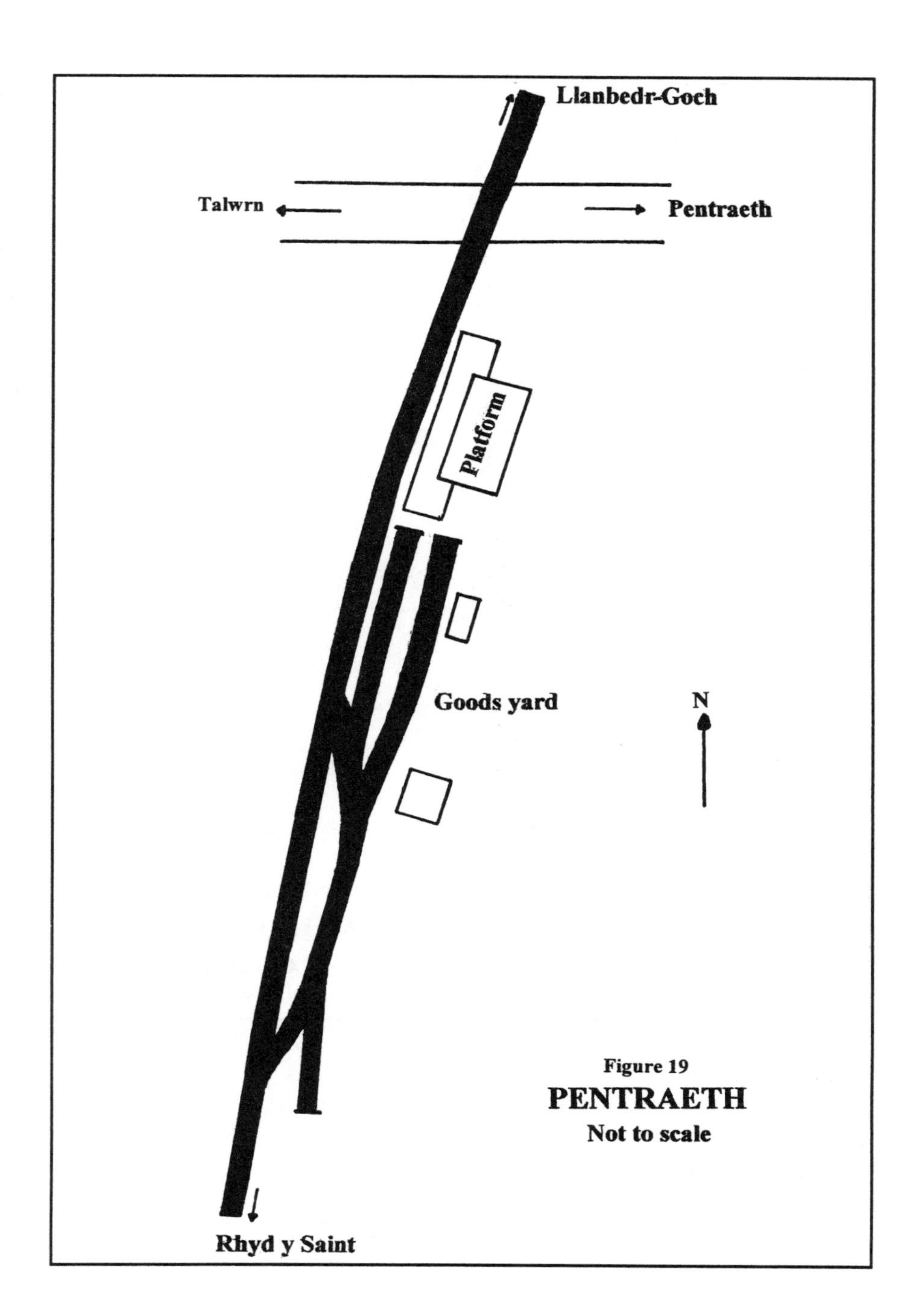

Figure 19
PENTRAETH
Not to scale

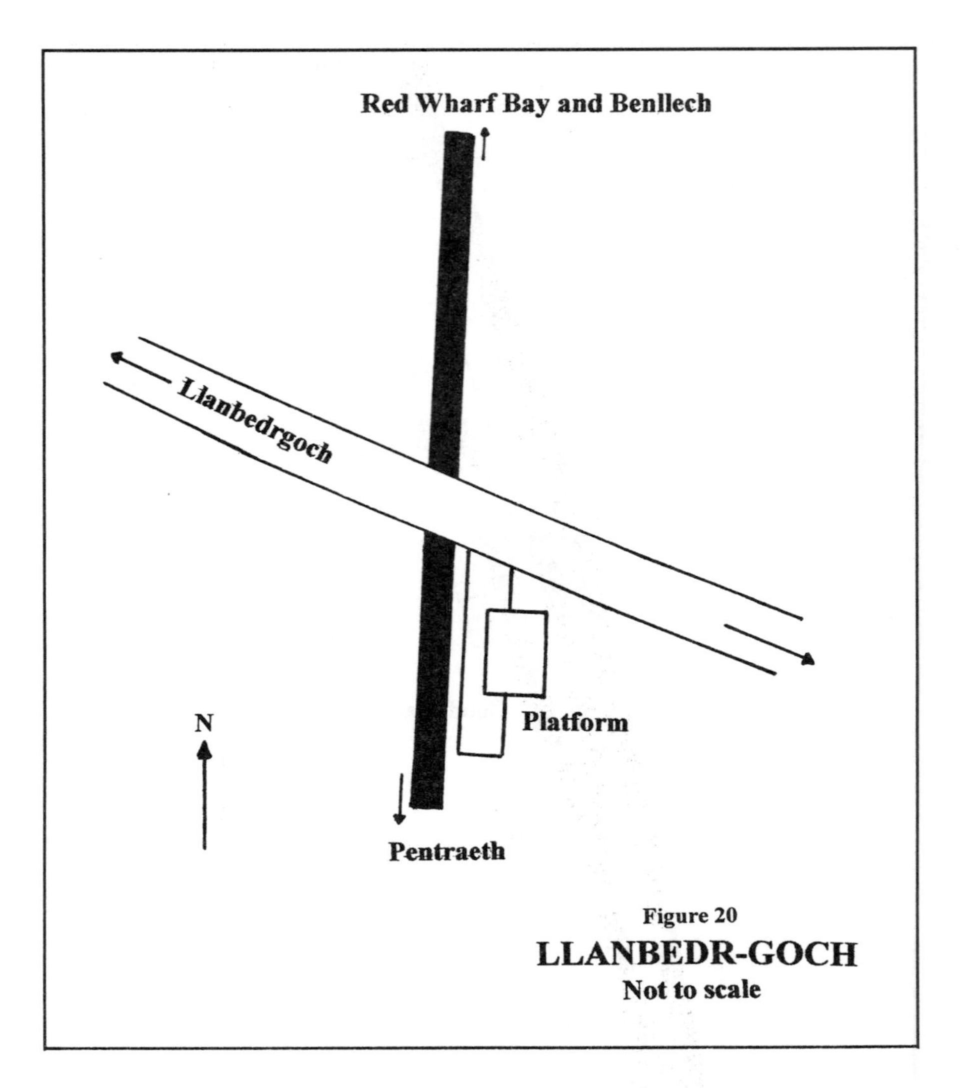

Figure 20
LLANBEDR-GOCH
Not to scale

Llanbedr-goch (Grid Reference SH 520 805)
Llanbedr-goch station (Figure 20) was a small halt (very similar to Ceint and Rhyd y Saint), opened on 24 May 1909. It was a conditional halt with a platform and hut on the Up side, and no goods yard. It was 6.18 miles (9.8 km) from Pentre Berw. After the closure of the line to regular passenger traffic in 1930, the site was cleared.

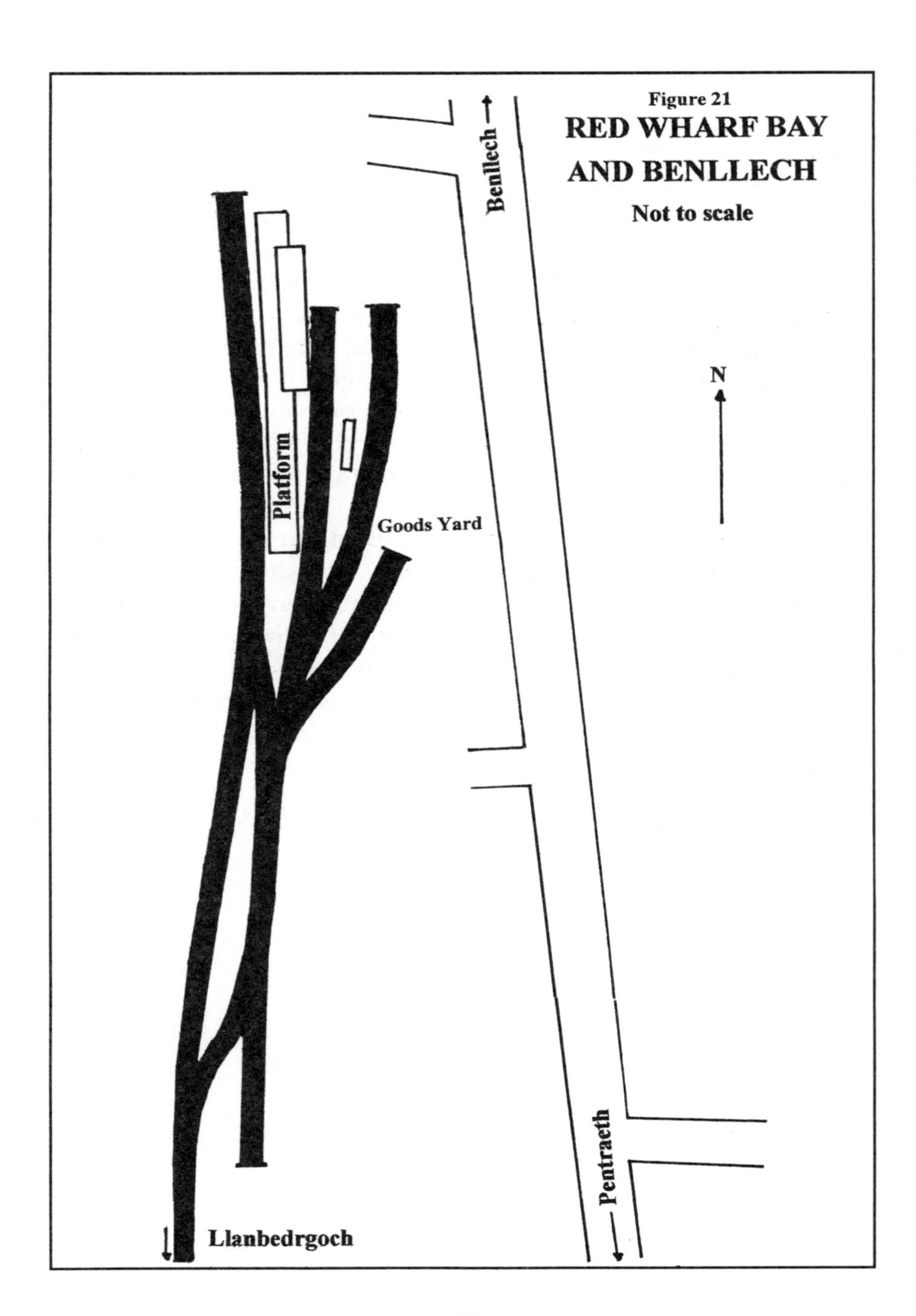
Figure 21
RED WHARF BAY
AND BENLLECH
Not to scale
Benllech
N
Platform
Goods Yard
Pentraeth
Llanbedrgoch

Red Wharf Bay and Benllech (Grid Reference SH 522 813)
This station (Figure 21) was the terminus for the line, and was opened on 24 May 1909. It was 6.62 miles (10.6 km) from Pentreberw, and passenger trains would take 21 minutes to cover that distance. The platform was initially 260 ft. long (although later reduced in length). It had a waiting room, booking office, toilets etc, and was permanently staffed. It also had a goods yard with 3 sidings and a loop. In its heyday, it was a busy station handling various goods, including livestock, coal, timber; it even had a crane. The goods yard had a loading gauge and a platelayer's hut (see Appendix). The approach to the station had a signal, the only one on the line. There were two ground frames to control the points. The station closed in 1950, and the buildings demolished some years later.

Soon after the railway reached Benllech in 1909 a local businessman started working a nearby limestone quarry and a lime kiln was built near the station. The intention was probably to transport the finished product (lime) by rail. However, the venture was short-lived since the cost of carrying the limestone to the kiln by horse and cart was too high. The kiln was subsequently used for other purposes and was later converted into a house and remains so today.

Chapter 5
OTHER ANGLESEY RAILWAY SCHEMES

These fall into two categories: proposed schemes which were never built (Figure 22), and those which were actually built and existed for a certain period of time.

PROPOSED SCHEMES THAT WERE NEVER BUILT

An Act of Parliament which received Royal Assent on 9 June 1812 granted permission to build a railway from Penrhynmawr (near Pentreberw) in the parish of Llanfihangel Ysgeifiog (Grid Reference SH 470 728) to Red Wharf in the parish of Llanbedrgoch. The proposals also included a dock at Red Wharf. This was the first proposed railway in Anglesey. The purpose of the line was said to be the transport of coal and limestone. There was at that time a coal mine near Pentreberw and the potential to export coal was being considered. The railway would probably have used horse-drawn wagons as did many industrial railways of this period. Various local worthies were connected to the scheme, such as the Honourable Berkeley Paget, Plas Newydd (MP for Anglesey, 1807-1820) and Holland Griffith, Carreglwyd. The railway was never built, although strangely, the Pentreberw to Red Wharf Line would follow a similar path nearly 100 years later.

In 1858, a scheme was proposed for the construction of a railway from Gaerwen through Llangefni to Amlwch and on to Cemaes and Llanrhuddlad and finally to Valley, where it would rejoin the main line. Part of this scheme, of course, was built as the Anglesey Central Railway, but the remainder came to nothing. A 4.24 mile (6.78 km) branch from Rhosgoch on the Central Anglesey Line to Cemaes, proposed in 1865, was never built. Extending the Anglesey Central Railway from Amlwch to Porth Amlwch (also

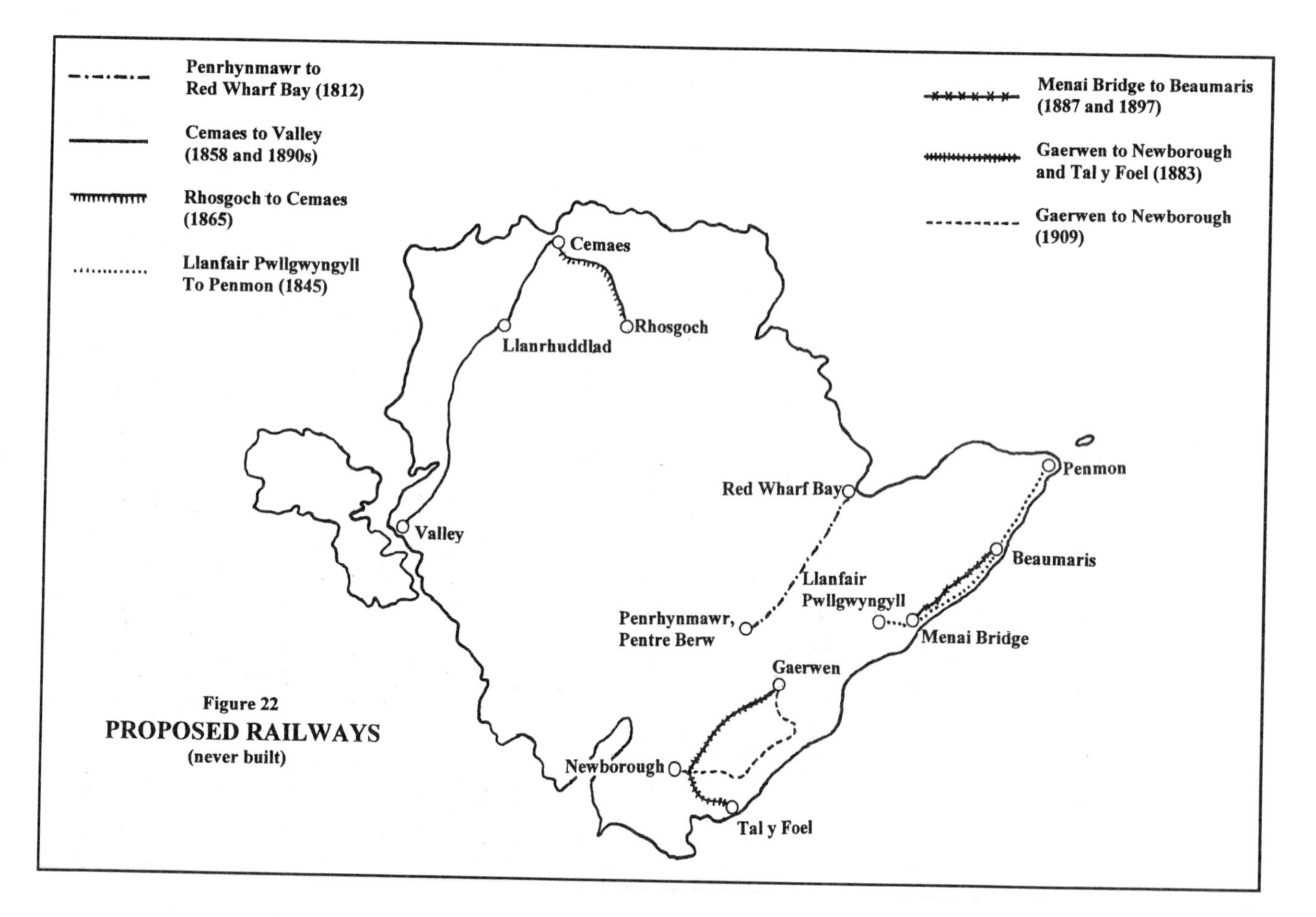

Figure 22
PROPOSED RAILWAYS
(never built)

proposed in 1865) never materialised either. In the 1890s, there was further talk of a railway between Amlwch and Valley, but it seems there was little support for this venture.

The popular resort town of Beaumaris was never served by a railway, although a number of schemes were considered. As early as 1845, a railway from Llanfair Pwllgwyngyll through Beaumaris and on to Penmon was proposed, but the scheme came to nothing. In 1880, a steam tramway to Beaumaris was proposed but not built. In 1887, the LNWR considered the possibility of a branch line to Beaumaris, but it is said that the scheme was abandoned due to engineering problems near the proposed Beaumaris station. In 1897, a line between Menai Bridge and Beaumaris was proposed by the LNWR. This was dropped in favour of an electric tramway from Llanfair Pwllgwyngyll to Beaumaris; this scheme was backed by a company from Halifax and would have involved building an electricity generating station, but the proposal was turned down by the authorities in June 1898. This followed a public inquiry conducted at Beaumaris Town Hall; there were numerous objections to the scheme and the proposals were turned down, largely on account of the narrowness of the road.

In 1883, an Anglesey and Caernarfon Direct Railway was proposed. The scheme proposed the building of a railway from Gaerwen to Caernarfon via Newborough and a ferry crossing). According to plans drawn up in November 1883, the line was to begin at the Gaerwen LNWR station and end at a pier near Tal y Foel, a total distance of 7.38 miles (11.81 km). In 1884, an alternative scheme (Anglesey and Caernarfon Direct No.2) was proposed; this railway was to follow a similar route and come within about 0.5 miles (0.8 km) of Newborough (at Grid Reference SH 433 653). Neither scheme received Parliamentary approval.

In 1909, the South Anglesey Light Railway of 8½ miles (13.6 km) from Gaerwen to Brynsiencyn and Newborough was proposed. The line was surveyed and plans produced; these plans show the line was to end 0.2 mile (0.3 km) from Newborough square (Grid Reference SH 426 624) and there was to be a pier (for a ferry crossing) near Cae Oerwaedd, Brynsiencyn (Grid Reference SH 495 665). The scheme was not approved and was never constructed.

ACTUAL RAILWAYS

These are railways used for an industrial purpose and not used by the public for passenger or freight purposes.

Mynydd Parys

This was a narrow gauge railway, only about 300 yards (275m) long, which ran from a smelting works to Porth Amlwch (Grid Reference SH 448 933). It was opened in 1833-34, but when the works closed, the track was removed.

There was at one time the intention to build a railway from the mines themselves to the port. In 1828, well-known engineer Charles Vignoles had surveyed the area and proposed that a railway could be built for £6300. His plans were never implemented.

Porthamel Quarry

This was a narrow gauge railway in the Brynsiencyn area about 0.5 mile (0.8 km) long running from a quarry (Grid Reference SH 508 678) to a pier (Grid Reference SH 507 673). The track was removed and no traces remain.

Porth Wen Brickworks

This brickworks lies on the north coast of Anglesey between Amlwch and Cemaes. There was an incline from the works at sea level up to a headland from where a tramway (2ft 6 in gauge) ran to a clay pit (Grid Reference SH 402 946). When the brickworks closed the track was removed.

Tan Dinas Quarry

At this quarry near Llanddona, a tramway (2ft gauge) ran from the quarry face to a pier (Grid Reference SH 583 820). The tramway was opened in 1928, and the quarry closed in 1956. The track was said to be in place in 1964.

Flagstaff Quarry

At this quarry near Penmon (Grid Reference SH 635 807) there was a fairly extensive 3ft gauge system with one locomotive connecting the quarry with a mill, kilns and a jetty. The quarry closed in 1941, but the track and locomotive are said to have remained until 1963 when the site was cleared.

Headland Quarry

At this quarry near Penmon (Grid Reference SH 635 815), a 3ft gauge railway system (with five locomotives) connected two quarries to a pier. The quarry was closed in 1966.

Penmon Park Quarries

At this quarry near Penmon (Grid Reference 628 805) a 3ft 6in gauge incline connected the quarry to a jetty. The incline passed under a road. A 0-4-0ST locomotive built in 1884 was used. This quarry closed in 1910.

Holyhead Breakwater and Quarry

The Holyhead Breakwater (Figure 10), which is 1.48 miles (2.38 km) long, was constructed between 1845 and 1873. The contractors, J. and C. Rigby used a wide gauge railway (See Appendix) to transport stone from a quarry (Grid Reference SH 227 833) to build the breakwater. Wide gauge was favoured because of the massive pieces of rock which were to be transported. Different 0-4-0WT locomotives were used, and a locomotive shed was located near Soldiers' Point (Grid Reference SH 235 836). A wide gauge line also ran towards Holyhead harbour at Salt Island; this was used for the transportation of construction materials for the Breakwater and, during the 1860s, it was used in the construction of the inner harbour. In 1902, the quarry and one locomotive were purchased by William Wild and Sons and the 7ft 0¼in line used for a time. The line on the breakwater was re-laid as a standard gauge line in 1913. The wide gauge line to Holyhead harbour was later removed and converted to a road. The track along the length of the breakwater is now used for maintenance; if the breakwater is damaged by bad weather building materials can be transported to the appropriate location.

Chapter 6
THE HOLYHEAD MAIN LINE NOW

Although the Bangor to Holyhead main line has remained intact and still carries a number of train services, the stations have undergone a number of changes. Gone are the days when substantial freight traffic passed through the Anglesey stations and the sidings have been largely uprooted. In this chapter are described some of the locations where interesting features of the line can be observed. Grid References are given for these locations; an ordnance survey map would, therefore, prove extremely useful.

Britannia Bridge

On the Anglesey side of the Britannia Bridge, remains of barracks used to house construction workers are still visible. Having parked in a large lay-by on the road between Menai Bridge and Llanfair Pwllgwyngyll (Grid Reference SH 541 717), follow a path which leads to the Menai Strait. Follow the signs and you will pass near to the remains of the barracks in the shadow of the bridge itself. Here, you are almost directly under the bridge and can appreciate its enormity. Following the path further will take you nearer to the Anglesey entrance to the bridge near the Carreg Brân Hotel. The cemetery at Llanfair Pwllgwyngyll church is only a short walk from here; in the churchyard can be seen a memorial to those who died during the construction of the bridge and its subsequent rebuilding. The memorial is clearly visible from the church gate. A short walk up the narrow road from this point takes you back to the main road and the lay-by is about 0.4 miles (0.6 km) from here. Having crossed the Britannia bridge to the mainland side, leave the dual carriageway by the first slip road. Turn left at the roundabout and almost immediately take a left turn. Follow the road for 0.3 mile (0.5 km) and park near a veterinary surgery.

From here, walk along a public footpath for a short distance before reaching the bridge. Here can be found a section of Stephenson's original tube, clearly showing its cellular construction. From this point, continue further down the path towards the Straits; on the right hand side are the remains of a fractured hydraulic press (used to raise Stephenson's tubes) mounted on a stone plinth.

Llanfair Pwllgwyngyll (Grid Reference SH 526 716)
Llanfair Pwllgwyngyll station is situated in the centre of the village and there is ample parking nearby. After the station closed in 1964, the goods yard was dismantled. The station was reopened to passenger traffic in the wake of the disastrous Britannia Bridge fire in 1970. The former goods yard site was a derelict eyesore for a number of years until the Pringle shop was built on the site in the 1980s. The Station building remains, and is in good condition thanks to the efforts of the Pringle company who restored it in 1994. The building is not currently in use. There is a footbridge between the two platforms. The crossover between the Up and Down lines has disappeared.

Gaerwen (Grid Reference SH 485 708)
There is sufficient parking space on either side of the level crossing. Gaerwen station closed in 1964, but signal box number 1 is still in place and in use. It is the only one of the main line stations to have closed permanently. The platforms have long disappeared, but the cross-over between the Up and Down lines is still in place, as is the connection with the Amlwch line. The goods yard is now occupied by an agricultural supplies company, and also houses a small coal yard. Some old-fashioned semaphore signals can be seen on either side of the level crossing. See also Chapter 7.

Tunnels
A short distance south of Bodorgan station are the only two tunnels on the Holyhead line (Grid References SH 400 697 and SH 396 698). The tunnel entrance can be viewed from a bridge carrying a very minor road over the railway (Grid Reference SH

405 695). It is preferable to leave the car and walk along this road as it is extremely narrow. However, it is well worth the short walk since a good view of the entrance to the largest tunnel can be had from here. Old OS maps refer to this tunnel as the Cip y Gwynt tunnel, although officially it is named Bodorgan No.1, the smaller tunnel being Bodorgan No.2. A good view can also be had from the bridge crossing the B4422 (Grid Reference SH 391 700). The track is very straight between these two bridges and there is a downward gradient towards Malltraeth. From here it is possible to see through both tunnels and the bridge (Grid Reference SH 405 695) can be seen in the distance.

Bodorgan (Grid Reference SH 387 702)
Bodorgan station is situated in a quiet rural location on a minor road (Grid Reference SH 387 702) not far from Bethel. There is ample room to park on the road outside the station. The goods yard is now in private hands, and the main station building (on the Up side) appears to be used as a house. There is no crossover between the Up and Down lines. It is possible (with appropriate care) to walk across the track from the Up platform to the Down platform.

Tŷ Croes (Grid Reference SH 348 724)
Tŷ Croes station stands on a junction on a minor road in a very rural location (Grid Reference SH 348 724) near a small village called Bryn Du. There is parking space near this junction. The goods yard is used for other purposes and is presumably in private hands. The signal box (still in use) stands by the level crossing. The Up and Down platforms are on opposite sides of the level crossing. A small fragment of the goods yard can still be seen on the Up side, opposite the Down platform. Two old-fashioned semaphore signals (see Appendix) remain, one for each line.

Rhosneigr (Grid Reference SH 328 738)
The station stands in a semi-rural location on the minor road leading from Llanfaelog to Rhosneigr (turn left opposite Llanfaelog church if approaching from the Aberffraw direction).

The station is 0.8 miles (1.3 km) from the church. Turn up the first of two tracks leading to the station (the one immediately *before* the bridge carrying the track over the road). This leads you to the Up platform where the 1953 building can still be seen, albeit in a bricked-up and derelict state. A small brick shelter is the only other building on this platform. On the Down platform, there remains no trace of the 1953 building and a bus-stop type shelter is the only structure on it. The station-master's house, now presumably in private hands, is still in place behind the Down platform.

Valley (Grid Reference SH 292 792)
The station is situated on the road to Trearddur Bay (turn left at the traffic lights if approaching from the Bangor direction). The main station building on the Up side is still largely intact, but appears to be boarded up. A small shelter remains on the Down side. A crossover remains on the Holyhead side of the station. The former goods yard seems to be used as a coal yard. The signal box (not the original box, judging by its condition) stands next to the level crossing, and there are two semaphore signals (see Appendix) on opposite sides of the crossing. A few hundred yards outside the station, on the Rhosneigr side, is a series of sidings, some of which are used in connection with Wylfa nuclear power station. This facility has a crane, and has also been used to turn around locomotives. There is a road entrance to these sidings, on the A5 about 0.2 miles (0.3 km) outside Valley.

Holyhead
After reaching Holyhead on the A5, turn left over the railway bridge (Grid Reference SH 248 820) and then right into Victoria Road. From this bridge, looking towards the harbour, can be seen the railway station and sidings. Looking towards Valley, there are more sidings and a signal box. A few hundred yards from here was the site of the first Holyhead station. A little further on the Up side is a tall derelict brick-built building and a large rusty tank – both remnants of better days.

Continue along Victoria Road and turn left into Prince of Wales

Road. From here Admiralty Pier and Admiralty Arch (Grid Reference SH 253 829) can be seen on the right. No railway tracks now reach as far as this point.

Continue along Prince of Wales Road and Newry Beach and take a left turn (Grid Reference SH 241 832) onto a minor road leading to Holyhead Breakwater Country Park. On this road once stood the wide-gauge railway line from Holyhead Mountain quarry (Chapter 2).

Chapter 7
THE ANGLESEY CENTRAL RAILWAY NOW

It is 40 years since the closure of the Central Anglesey Railway (apart from its use by the Octel company). Hopes were raised at various times that it could reopen, particularly so during the 1990s, when ambitious plans were made to open the line as a heritage railway. However, its future is rather uncertain at present. This chapter attempts to reveal how the interested observer can see how the line and its stations have changed in the last 40 years. Although one must not trespass on the line, there are a considerable number of places where features of the line can be observed. These will be described in conjunction with Grid References; an ordnance survey map will, therefore, be very useful.

Gaerwen (Grid Reference SH 485 708)
After parking near the station, walk up a minor road approximately 0.3 miles (0.5 km). This road crosses over the Amlwch line (Grid Reference SH 480 707); from this point it is possible to see the sorry state of the track. Much of the line is in this condition.

Pentreberw (Grid Reference SH 471 726)
Pentreberw station is located opposite a garden centre. This station was the first to close on the Anglesey Central Line, shortly after the Red Wharf Bay line was finally closed. The station building and former goods yard are now in private hands and are used as a coal business. Near the station, work on the new A55 in 2000 necessitated the construction of a short tunnel under the new road and a new track was laid. This can be viewed by turning right along a minor road a few hundred yards down the hill from the garden centre (Grid Reference SH 470 728). See also Chapter 8.

Llangefni (Grid Reference SH 456 758)

Llangefni station is at the top end of the High Street, not far from the appropriately named *Railway Inn*. The station closed in 1964 and the station buildings have been in private hands for some time. The former station yard houses a shop, but most of it is in the hands of the council and is used as a car park. The loop near the platform has been removed. Standing on the metal footbridge which passes over the railway (Grid Reference SH 457 758), the overgrown state of the track bed and parts of the former station are all too apparent. A few yards up the hill from the footbridge can be seen the entrance to a sloping track which was used to load livestock onto freight trains. The track can be very clearly seen from the footpath in parts of the wooded area known as Nant y Glyn (*The Dingle*). This area can be reached by a path from the station yard car park. The railway passes through Nant y Glyn and crosses over the Afon Cefni a number of times; bridges of various descriptions can be seen. The bridge which stands a few hundred yards north of the station appears to be in a poor state. There is a footpath passing under it and it can clearly be seen that parts of the structure have fallen through. There is also evidence that vandals have lit fires on the bridge. At the far end of Nant y Pandy, the path enters a clearing where a ruined building (*Pandy*) stands (Grid Reference SH 453 766). Near this building, the path passes under another railway bridge. From here, the track continues towards Llangwyllog.

Llangwyllog (Grid Reference SH 436 790)

Llangwyllog was a small rural station situated on the minor road between Bodffordd and the road connecting Amlwch and Llangefni (B5111). The track can be viewed from the bridge which carries the road over the railway (Grid Reference SH 438 788). The station buildings themselves (now a private residence) cannot be viewed from this point.

Llannerch-y-medd (Grid Reference SH 417 840)
Llannerch-y-medd station is located in the centre of the village. If approaching from Llangefni, carry straight on at the mini roundabout in the centre of the village. About 100 yards further on, turn left into the station yard where there is ample parking in the former goods yard. The station building (albeit bricked up) remains. The platform is also in place. The Stationmaster's house (*Station House*) stands high up on the street just outside the station yard. There are tentative plans to develop the station at present, including a railway heritage centre.

Rhos-goch (Grid Reference SH 410 894)
To reach Rhos-goch, turn left about 2 miles (3 km) north of Llannerch-y-medd. Just outside Rhos-goch, the railway passes over a minor road (Grid Reference SH 413 887). This bridge appears to be in a dire condition since parts of its bottom appear to have fallen through. In Rhos-goch itself the railway travels under the road next to the Rhos-goch Hotel (also known as *The Ring*). Looking over the bridge wall towards the north reveals remnants of a flight of steps leading down to the track (presumably for inspection purposes). The station building itself is a short distance from this bridge, but is now in private hands and cannot be viewed from the bridge.

Amlwch (Grid Reference SH 442 928)
The station entrance was formerly in Salem Street. During the 1970s, however, the building of a by-pass road meant that some of the station buildings were lost, although one corrugated iron goods shed remained for a number of years but now seems to have disappeared. A few remains of the station (e.g. the edge of the platform) can still be seen in the overgrown site between the by-pass and Salem Street (Figure 23). The site of the station can conveniently be viewed from a road bridge in Llwynon Road which passes over the track (Grid Reference SH 438 927). The line from Rhos-goch passes under the bridge and continues towards Octel, with a small loop remaining. A lever to control the points can be seen at the side of the track. The Octel line crosses the by-

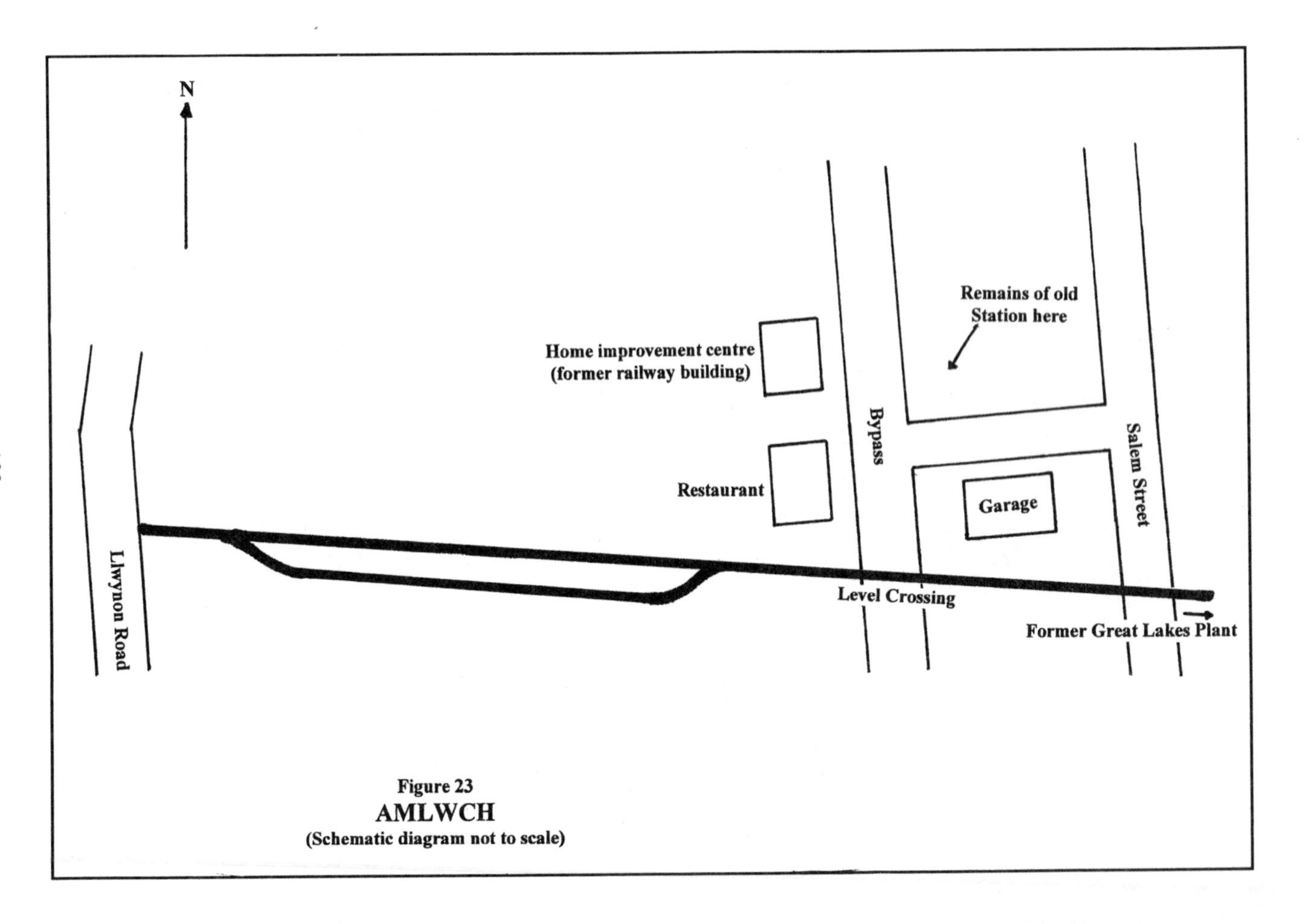

Figure 23
AMLWCH
(Schematic diagram not to scale)

pass and Salem Street (Grid Reference SH 443 928) where, in both cases, the crossing gates have now been removed and replaced by a fence. A little further along, the line crosses two more streets (Grid references SH 445 929 and SH 446 931) where the original crossing gates are still in place. The line then proceeds to the Octel site (more recently known as the Great Lakes company) where the track bed appears to have been covered with chippings and may have been used as a parking ground before the plant closed in January 2004. (Grid Reference SH 446 936). In June 2004, the Amercian company, Canatxx Energy, bought the Great Lakes site for use as part of a natural gas project, and the same company was said to be interested in purchasing the former Shell site at Rhos-goch for the construction of a gas-fuelled electricity power station. The Canatxx company had previously expressed an interest in the Rhos-goch site in 1995. One can but wonder whether these developments may require the use of the Central Anglesey Line once more.

Chapter 8
THE RED WHARF BAY LINE: 50 YEARS ON

The working life of the Red Wharf Bay line was not a long one: the track was finally removed during a six month period in 1953. So what remains of the line now? One must bear in mind that the line is now in private hands and must not be trespassed upon. Nevertheless, there are public footpaths that cross or follow the line and others that are in close proximity to it. The purpose of this chapter is to draw attention to some features of the line which can still be observed. These features will be described in conjunction with Grid References; consequently an ordnance survey map will be extremely useful.

Pentreberw (Grid Reference SH 471 726)
This station has been in private hands for a number of years, and in the very recent past changes have been caused by the building of the A55 dual carriageway just north of the station. When travelling through Pentreberw towards Llangefni, after passing a garden centre on your left, take a right turn on to a minor road (Grid Reference SH 469 727). After passing a cluster of houses, the road passes under the A55 and, immediately afterwards, the road widens slightly and there is sufficient room to park on the left hand side. From this point you should be able to see where the Amlwch line passes under the A55. The rails and ballast are new at this point. The Amlwch line then passes under a bridge near the parking place. From this point walk along a narrow road with a high wall on the right hand side for a few hundred yards. When the road curves to the right, you will be able to see the characteristic red and purple brickwork of a bridge (SH 471 729). This is the typical design used on the Red Wharf Bay line. The purple coping stones bear the name *W. Hancock & Co, Buckley,*

Flintshire. Looking over the bridge towards Ceint, the former track bed is extremely overgrown and hardly visible. Looking over the bridge towards Pentreberw is impossible since a car-breaker's yard has been built on the track bed. Sadly, there is no more to see at Pentreberw.

Turn back on to the A5 and continue in the direction of Gaerwen, but after approximately 0.2 mile (0.3 km), turn left on to a minor road which leads to Ceint. After 0.6 mile (0.9 km), a public footpath starts on the left near a couple of houses (Grid Reference SH 478 730). The path leads past a derelict 15th century church and cemetery (Llanfihangel Ysgeifiog) and, eventually, after 0.5 mile (0.8 km) passes over a solid-looking single-arched bridge (Grid Reference SH 473 735) under which passed the Red Wharf Bay line. Within yards of this bridge is a three-arched footbridge. Both bridges appear to be in good condition. The track bed itself is very clearly discernable with old concrete fencing posts on both sides (but no fencing wire). The track bed is not overgrown, probably due to grazing by animals. About 0.3 mile (0.5 km) to the north of this point can be seen another single-arched bridge.

Ceint (Grid Reference SH 488 748)
Figure 17 shows the location of the station (SH 488 748). It is situated near a road junction where there is ample parking near a grass verge on the minor road from Pentre Berw. Walking up from the junction (about 25 metres) towards Llangefni, the road crosses over a bridge. The characteristic red and purple bricks can be seen forming the wall on both sides of the road. Looking over the wall on your left (the Pentreberw side) reveals that the flat raised area, which formed the station platform (and on which the station hut once stood), is still in place. Its brick construction is still apparent. A brick culvert also appears to be intact. Trees grow on the track bed, but it appears that sheep may play a part in keeping track bed growth to a minimum.

Eglwys Llanffinan
From Ceint drive towards Llangefni, but almost immediately turn to the right into a narrow unclassified road. After 0.6 mile (1.0 km)

there is an entrance to Llanffinan Church on your right. The Church (Grid Reference SH 496 755) can be reached along this rough track (which is also a public footpath). There is ample parking space in the vicinity of the church. To the right of the church the footpath continues through a gate into a field. In the distance can be seen Plas Penmynydd. The field slopes down towards the tiny Afon Ceint which can be crossed by a small bridge, and a stile leads on to the former track bed which is extremely overgrown and virtually impossible to explore.

Rhyd y Saint (Grid Reference SH 499 758)
Emerging from the rough track to Llanffinan Church, turn right back on to the minor road and continue for 0.2 mile (0.3 km). Then turn right down a narrow road (near a cluster of houses) and the site of the former Rhyd y Saint station is 0.4 mile (0.6 km) down this road (Grid Reference SH 499 758) This road becomes very narrow indeed and it may be advisable to find a parking space and walk down. There is no adequate parking space near the former station itself. The location of the station is easily found since it is below a bridge having the same red and purple bricks that have already been mentioned. Looking over the bridge (in the Ceint direction) the flat raised area of the platform can be seen. The track bed itself at this point is fairly overgrown, with some quite large trees being present. Along the track to the south of the bridge is a platelayers' hut.

Pentraeth (Grid Reference SH 518 753)
Pentraeth station stood on an exposed elevated spot about 0.3 miles (0.5 km) from the village on the road to Talwrn (turn left in the centre of Pentraeth). Until the 1960s, a bridge crossed over the road to carry the railway; the bridge support (albeit somewhat cracked) remains on the right hand side of the road, but any structure on the left has been destroyed by road widening. In the vicinity of the bridge the track bed cannot be examined as it is extremely overgrown. A road leads towards the site of the former station on which a number of houses were built some years ago.

About 0.5 miles (0.8 km) outside Pentraeth, on the minor road which leads to Llanffinan (Grid Reference SH 517 778), the location of a former bridge can clearly be seen. Although the top of the bridge has been removed, the supports are still in place.

A little outside Pentraeth on the A5025 towards Benllech can be seen a three arch brick bridge carrying a footpath over the railway (Grid Reference SH521 789). The bridge lies at the far corner of a field to which there does not appear to be any access. However, a little further on (Grid Reference SH 520 793), there is an identical bridge in a field through which a public footpath passes. The track bed to the north of this bridge has been filled in, but to the south the track bed is more clearly visible. On the opposite side of the road from this field (Grid Reference SH 520 794) the characteristic red and purple brickwork of a bridge can be seen. This bridge carried the road over the railway. The brickwork on the opposite side of the road have disappeared due to road works in the 1960s.

Llanbedr-goch (Grid Reference SH 520 805)
About half a mile further along the A5025 towards Benllech (Grid Reference SH 520 802), lies a bridge which carried the old A5025 over the railway. This is partly obscured by trees and bushes. The north side of the bridge (made of regulation red and purple bricks) looks over a caravan site. The south side of the bridge is, unusually, made of bricks and metal railings.

Just across the A5025 road from this point (and clearly indicated as a public footpath), there is a small gate leading to a field. Having entered the field, follow the hedge (on your left) for a few yards and suddenly the former track bed comes into view and extends for some distance until it reaches a caravan site. This part of the track bed is part of a field where sheep graze and growth is kept to a minimum.

A few hundred yards further towards Benllech lies a junction (close to a house called *Llain Delyn*). Turn left and follow this road for a few hundred yards and the evidence of a bridge is obvious, in the form of the red and purple bricks on both sides of the road (Grid Reference SH 520 805). Looking over the wall on the left side of the road shows that the track bed is now a caravan park – this is where the station platform used to be. Looking over the wall on the right towards Benllech shows that the track bed is still visible and less overgrown than in some locations. There is a public footpath leading into the field on the Benllech side of the road. However, this does not permit access to the track bed.

Benllech (Grid Reference SH 522 813)
The former station and goods yard stood close to a road junction just outside the village (Grid Reference SH 522 813). The station house is the only remaining visible feature of the station. Two small lay-bys can be found on the A5025 at this point. In one of them, a large metal gate, firmly padlocked, guards the entrance to what used to be the goods yard. In the distance can be seen a large building, but this is much more recent than the railway. There is no access to the site which appears to be overgrown and probably unused at present.

APPENDIX
TECHNICAL TERMS

(Most, although not all, the terms in this Appendix are referred to in the text).

Aspinall Class 27 Locomotive — Locomotives with separate tenders of 3F 0-6-0 specification designed by John Aspinall for the Lancashire and Yorkshire Railway. Nearly 500 were built between 1889 and 1918, and 300 remained in service with the LMSR in 1945. Only one has been preserved.

Ballast — Coarse chippings used as bedding material for sleepers and rails.

Bay platform — Railway platform with a cul-de-sac (e.g. at Gaerwen) which served as a starting point or terminus for a branch line.

Beeching Report — In 1963, the railways of Britain came under the control of the British Railways Board, and its first chairman was Dr Richard Beeching. It was his report that led to the closure of a few main lines and numerous unprofitable branch lines.

BR Standard Class Locomotives — When the Railways were nationalised in 1948, the network was using a vast assortment of different locomotives designed at various times by the different companies. It was decided to rationalise the locomotives into 12 different standard designs, known as *Standard Class* Locomotives under chief engineer Robert Riddles. Many were based on, and some were almost identical to, previous designs, particularly LMSR designs (see below).

BR Standard Class 2 Locomotive — Tender locomotive of 2MT 2-6-0 specification. These were the smallest of the British Railways tender locomotives. Over 60 were built between 1952 and 1956 and only four survive. It was almost identical to the earlier LMSR 2MT 2-6-0 designed by George Ivatt and first produced in 1946. Over 120 of these were built between 1946 and 1953; only seven have survived.

BR Standard Class 4 Locomotive — Tank locomotive of 4MT 2-6-4T specification. Built between 1951 and 1957, about 150 were produced.

The design owed much to the previous LMSR designs of Sir William A. Stanier and Charles Fairburn.

BR Standard Class 5 Locomotive — Tender locomotive of 5MT 4-6-0 specification. About 170 of these powerful locomotives were built between 1951 and 1957; only 5 have survived. It was based on earlier LMSR designs of Sir William A. Stanier, the 'Black Five', of which 840 were built between 1934 and 1951.

BR Standard Class 7P6F 4-6-2 Locomotive — The Britannia Pacific locomotive was designed by Robert Riddles and 55 were built between 1951 and 1954. Only two have survived. The term 'Pacific' simply describes the 4-6-2 wheel configuration.

British Railways — The railway network formed in 1948, when the separate railway companies were nationalised and known as British Rail after 1965. This continued until the privatisation of the network in 1996 when a plethora of railway companies ran services, along track belonging to Railtrack (later Network Rail).

Chair — Clamp fixed on sleepers which holds the rails in place.

Classification of Locomotives — Locomotives are classified according to their role: P (hauling passenger trains), F (freight) or MT (mixed traffic, i.e. passenger and freight). Additionally, a number denotes the power of the locomotive, ranging from 0P to 8P, 0F to 9F, and 2MT to 7MT. Consequently, a locomotive designated as 2MT is a mixed traffic locomotive, of fairly low power.

Cutting — An area which has been excavated during construction of a line so as to reduce the gradients.

Diesel Multiple Unit (DMU) — Trains with Diesel engines built into the coaches themselves. There are driving cabs at the outer ends of the coaches at each end of the train. When the coaches are coupled up, control cables enable the driver in the leading cab to control all the Diesel engines.

Down line — On a twin track line, the Down line is the track that would take you away from London (i.e. towards Holyhead, Amlwch etc). Therefore, on Gaerwen station, for example, the Down line is on the left as a train travels towards Holyhead, and the Down platform is on the left. On a twin track line, the trains normally travel on the left (like cars on the roads). This definition can be extended to single track lines: at Rhos-goch, for example, the platform is described as being on the Down side as it is on the left as a train travels to Amlwch.

Fairlie locomotive — Tank locomotives of unusual appearance, resembling two engines stuck together and facing in opposite directions. The *Progress* used by contractors on the Central Anglesey line was designated as 0-4-4-0T. This type of locomotive was designed by Robert Fairlie. The Ffestiniog Railway (Porthmadog) is still using a Fairlie locomotive named *David Lloyd George*.

Ground frame — A lever frame located at ground (i.e. track) level, and used to operate points etc.

Ivatt Class 2MT 2-6-2T locomotive — This tank locomotive was introduced in 1946 and considered to be one of the best branch line locomotives ever produced in Britain, skilfully designed by LMSR designer George Ivatt; about 130 were built mostly for British Railways, but only 4 are thought to have survived. They were much used on the Amlwch branch line.

Lever frame — Set of levers for operating signals, points etc. A lever frame is often located in a signal box, but on branch lines they were sometimes to be found on the platform.

Light engine — A locomotive travelling alone without carriages or rolling stock.

Light Railway — A railway designed and built for light traffic, e.g. the Pentreberw to Red Wharf Bay line. Light railways are not built to the same exacting specification as a normal railway, and normally operating restrictions would apply e.g. speed and locomotive power.

Locking Bars — Bars to lock points tightly so that they are not disturbed by passing trains.

LMSR — The London, Midland and Scottish Railway. Company formed in 1923 by the amalgamation of a number of smaller railway companies (including the LNWR). The 123 separate railway companies which existed before 1923 were reorganised into four new companies. The LMSR survived until nationalisation in 1948.

LMSR Princess Coronation Class 8P 4-6-2	This was a powerful passenger locomotive designed by the LMSR. Between 1937 and 1948, 38 were built but only 3 remain.
LMSR Royal Scot Class 7P 4-6-0	The Royal Scot was designed by the LMSR and about 70 were built between 1927 and 1930. Only 2 have survived.
LNWR	London and North Western Railway. It was absorbed into the LMSR in 1923. The LNWR was itself formed by the merger of the London and Birmingham Railway, the Grand Junction Railway and the Manchester and Birmingham Railway on 16 July 1846.
Motor Trains	See Push-pull operation.
Nationalisation	The British railway companies were nationalised (i.e. brought into state ownership) in 1948. Anglesey and north Wales were in the London Midland region of the newly created British Railways (British Rail from 1965).
Passing Loop	A loop of track on a line (usually a single track line) so that trains can pass each other. These will usually be at stations.
Platelayer	A man who inspects and repairs the railway track.
Push-pull operation	A type of train which was sometimes used on a single track line. The train can be driven in reverse and the driver can control the locomotive (using mechanical linkages or, later, vacuum control) from the end carriage thereby getting a proper view of the track. The fireman remains in the locomotive. Used on the Red Wharf Bay and Benllech line, occasionally on the Amlwch line. Also known as Motor Trains (or auto trains).
Rolling Stock	Passenger carriages or freight wagons.
Section	A length of line usually between two stations (or two signal boxes) where only one train is permitted to be at one time (for obvious safety reasons). On twin track railways (such as the Holyhead line), two trains are permitted in one section provided they are on separate tracks. The movement of trains is controlled by signalmen. There are elaborate procedures used to ensure the smooth and safe operation of the network e.g. signals and tokens.

Semaphore Signals	Old fashioned railway signals using moveable arms operated by wires from a signal box or from lever frames/ground frames.
Single Track	A railway where trains move in both directions along a single set of rails, e.g. the Amlwch and Red Wharf Bay branch lines.
Sleeper(s)	Wooden or reinforced concrete structures to support the rails. There are approximately 2000 sleepers per mile of track (1250 per km).
Standard gauge	Gauge is the distance between the inner edges of the rails. Standard gauge is 4 ft. 8½ in. (1435 mm). All Anglesey public railways were built to this specification. It is also used on most European and American railways and in many other parts of the world.
Tank Engine	A steam locomotive where the water and fuel are carried on the locomotive itself, as opposed to a separate tender. When a locomotive is described as 2-6-2T, the letter T denotes tank engine.
Terminus	Terminus is the station at the end of a line, e.g. Amlwch is the terminus of the Central Anglesey line.
Turntable	A device for turning locomotives (or rolling stock) around so that they face the other way. Often used on single track railways. Neither of the Anglesey branch lines was fitted with a turntable.
Twin track	A railway line having two parallel railway tracks, e.g. Chester to Holyhead main line.
Up line	On a twin track railway, the Up line is the one that would eventually take you to London. At Gaerwen station, for example, the Up line is the left hand line as the train passes towards Bangor and the Up platform is the platform on your left. On twin track railways trains normally run on the left (like cars on the road) This definition can be extended to single track lines: at Llangefni, for example, the station buildings are on the Up side because they are on your left as you travel to London.
Webb 1P 2-4-2T Locomotive	Tank Locomotive designed by Francis William Webb once Chief Mechanical Engineer of the LNWR.

Wheel arrangements

The usual system for describing wheel arrangements refers to to numbers of leading bogies – coupled driving wheels – trailing wheels. Thus 2-6-4 means 2 leading bogie wheels (nearest front of locomotive), 6 coupled driving wheels (large wheels) and 4 trailing wheels.

Wide gauge

A track gauge of 7ft 0¼in (2140 mm) as used on Isambard Kingdom Brunel's Great Western Railway (GWR) which ran from London to Bristol. It was said to give a smoother ride, but was too expensive. The GWR was eventually converted to standard gauge.